Bringing Home the Laundry

Bringing Home
the Laundry

*Effective Parenting for
College and Beyond*

Janis Brody, Ph.D.

Taylor Trade Publishing
Dallas, Texas

Designed by Janis Owens

Published by Taylor Publishing Company
1550 West Mockingbird Lane
Dallas, Texas 75235
www.taylorpub.com

Library of Congress Cataloging-in-Publication Data

Brody, Janis.
   Bringing home the laundry : effective parenting for college and beyond / Janis Brody.
      p. cm.
   ISBN 0-87833-184-0 (pbk.)
   1. College student orientation—United States.   2. College students—United States—Family
relationships.   3. Parent and child—United States.   I. Title.
LB2343.32 .B72 2000
378.1'98—dc21
                                                                              00-042586

10   9   8   7   6   5   4   3   2   1

Printed in the United States of America

This book is dedicated in loving memory to my father, Alan S. Brody—a change assister, who in his typical incredibly generous manner, ensured that I had a place to live on my college campus, and believed that I could be successful at whatever I chose to do.

ACKNOWLEDGMENTS

There are so many generous people without whom this book would not have been possible. First and foremost are the many college students and their parents who shared their feelings and hopes, and opened up their homes for the sake of research. I am grateful to my editor Camille Cline, my agent Todd Keithley, and Jane Dystel Literary Management for believing that this book has something important to say. Thanks to Daniel Greenberg for connecting me with Mr. Keithley. I am indebted to Rose Greenberg for her technical support, to my mom for storing my research data in a safe place, and to Deep Dutta for putting so much heart and soul into cartoons that had been planned for the book.

I am especially grateful to Ashley Novak, Liz Zach, and Yun Xian Ho, not just for their practical help, but also for their dedication to the project. I greatly appreciate the assistance of my other New York City research assistants: Joanna Lehman, Claira Kim, Brad Reid, Melissa Rampy, Ariel Harman, Janille Bageal, Emily Beichel, Karen Keyser, Helen Lim, Melita Loncar, Harrold Magny, Srisunee Riantongchana, Janet Liu, John Collins, Chin Pak, and Cynthia Przybylski.

Thank you to my talented friends Donna Cohen, Dr. Judith Schteingart, Dr. Jill Putterman, Dr. Henry Kronengold, Valery Simon, Dr. Ellie Ehrenfeld, and Sallie Raynor for their insightful feedback on parts of the book. Many thanks to Verna Brown for her support during my childhood years and her continued friendship. I want to acknowledge Dr. Phil Cowan for his guidance, and Dr. Joel Nigg and Dan Silver for their invaluable statistical assistance. I am also grateful for the support of Dr. Rhona Weinstein and Rosemary Hendrick, and the assistance of many University of California at Berkeley undergraduate students, especially Laurie and Ken Hutz. I want to extend a special thanks to Dr. Salvador Minuchin, Olga Silverstein, and Peggy Papp, who helped inspire my commitment to a family systems approach.

CONTENTS

FOREWORD

_____

_____

_____

The Book and the Research That Backs It Up

When your child leaves home for college it can be a time of many confusing emotions, including anxiety about what will happen to the relationship with your son or daughter whom you love and want to keep close. *Bringing Home the Laundry* is here to reassure you that your child's departure for college can mark the beginning of a deeply satisfying, exciting new phase in your parent-child relationship. This book will teach you how to reap the potential benefits of this period, by helping you:

- Feel less sad about your child's departure and worry less about his well-being.
- Express the pride and confidence in your child that she needs to flourish at school.
- Teach your child how to make sound life decisions.
- Give your child enough space so that when you call she'll be really happy to hear from you.
- Make your child's visits home so enjoyable that he'll be returning every summer.
- Enjoy the wonderful opportunities that this phase of life has to offer you.

These are just a few of the many themes that *Bringing Home the Laundry* explores. By the end of the book, you will be an expert in how to parent your college-aged child.

The book's reassurances and guidance are based on five years of research.

More than 140 college students and 200 of their parents responded to interview questions, as well as to written questionnaires. The in-person interviews with students and their parents were conducted separately. The parents graciously welcomed researchers into their homes, sharing their parental successes and failures, their joys and deepest fears.

The majority of the students who participated in the study were attending the University of California at Berkeley; the minority were at New York University; and a small sampling were from schools around the country contacted via E-mail. Most students were in their first or second year of college. The ethnic, religious, and socioeconomic backgrounds of the families were tremendously varied. Parents' professions ran the gamut from business executive to teacher to factory worker to FBI agent. In a few families, both parents had to work two jobs; in others, one parent was able to take care of the kids full-time. Students also demonstrated diversity: They included premeds, musicians, community activists, sorority and fraternity members, and jocks. Most students lived at school, but many still lived at home. Most families had two parents living together, but several were single-parent or step-parent homes.

The identity of each and every one of these families has been disguised and rendered anonymous in the telling of their stories. In some cases, quotes from different families were combined into a single identity. The book's conclusions and advice were drawn from both statistical analyses and qualitative review of the interview transcripts. The study selected families randomly to ensure accurate representation of the general population and, thus, statistically significant results.

The parents participating in the study longed to learn what their children had said in response to the same questions, but understood that all information was confidential. They said that talking about the college transition was helpful, but that they wished there were a book on the topic for them to read. You will get to hear what both students and parents had to say, as well as learn from their experiences. Unlike the participating families, you will have a book to guide you and let you know when you're on the right track.

INTRODUCTION

Bringing Home the Laundry

The following is a true story: Once a month, a bright college woman lugged a huge suitcase full of dirty clothes onto a crowded city bus, sat with it for over a hundred blocks of stopping and starting, then dragged it across town up and down curbs. Was she hoping to meet a special young man at a downtown laundromat? No. Was she conducting an experiment on how strangers react to a woman with a smelly suitcase? No. Was she bringing her laundry home? Yes.

The anecdote doesn't end here, however. You probably think that the mother happily did her daughter's laundry and sent her away with enough home-cooked meals to last until the next load. Quite the contrary. The daughter washed her own laundry, along with her mother's socks, in the basement of a big apartment building, and left with only a snack in her belly. When asked why this young co-ed, who had laundry facilities in the basement of her dorm, went through such travails to bring her laundry home, both mother and daughter answered that time and effort were saved. Why would two intelligent women earnestly give a seemingly bizarre response? Interviews with more than 140 college students and 200 of their parents revealed the answer: Families often fear that leaving home will weaken family bonds, so they strive to stay connected any way they can, even if it means going to incredible lengths to do it.

Fortunately, neither you nor your child has to drag laundry all over town or across state lines in order to be close. My research indicates that college gives families the chance to strengthen their bonds, and that positive family relationships help students adjust well to college. *Bringing Home the Laundry* will assist you in taking advantage of this window of opportunity; you can make a tense relationship with your child a happy one, and make a warm relationship even warmer. You may have trouble believing my assurance because our culture tells parents to "let go" of their college-aged children, as if all parenting ends when university begins. I'm happy to tell you that your parenting is just as important to your child as ever. Don't let go; just loosen your grip.

Don't let go; loosen your grip.

Loosening one's grip is like good kiteflying. Imagine that you're the kiteflyer and the kite is your child. The initial launching is often tricky: Is there enough wind? Is the kite angle right? Are you running fast enough? The launching phase resembles when you were learning to soothe and care for your newborn child who needed almost constant attention. As the kite lifts into the air (your child crawls and walks and talks), you feel a little tug on the kite string and you let out a little more line (giving your child more space to explore the world). As the kite climbs higher and higher, the tugs become more frequent; if you're holding the string controls loosely, the appropriate measure of string will roll off the ball with each tug, and the kite will continue to soar.

Then suddenly, you feel a powerful gust of wind coming from behind and you brace yourself (your child is about to leave for college). Now what do you do? The experienced kiteflyer will release a lot of string, while maintaining a grip on the line, and then enjoy watching the kite reach great heights. In other words, the child leaves home with the parents' blessing and support, and thus, succeeds in college. Just as the kiteflyer will feel pride in the heights that the kite reaches, so too should you, the parent, in assisting your child's university adjustment.

A loose grip is much better than letting go, which would cause the kite to drift away and get stuck in a tree. The typical tendency of parents faced with having their children leave for college, however, is not letting go, but rather holding on too tightly. This means that they try to maintain the relationship similarly to how it was during the high school years. In kiteflying terms, a tight, unwavering grip will make the string become very taut, restraining the kite from soaring upward, and possibly, causing it to crash land. In family terms, the parent-child relationship can become tense and the child may have difficulty adjusting to college.

Too tight a parental grip can lead to family and college adjustment problems.

Why do many parents tend to hold on too tightly when their children leave for college? Resistance is the natural response to impending change; the familiar feels safer than the unfamiliar. All transitions are scary, even the ones we look forward to. There are many clichés, including the one of the nervous bridegroom on his wedding day. For parents faced with their child's college transition, fear of the unknown can take on many forms, including:

- Worrying that the quality of the time they spend with their child won't be as good as it used to be.
- Fearing that any existing relationship conflict will never have a chance to be resolved.
- Being concerned that their child will have difficulty adjusting to college.
- Panicking that if their child gets into trouble, they won't be able to help.

The good news is that if parents make sure to loosen their grip, then the exact opposite of these parental fears will result: The quality of time spent together will be *better* than ever before. Pre-existing tensions will be eased, and parents will be able to give their children the support they need to succeed in college. The bad news is that if parents respond to their fear of change by holding on too tightly, then their fears may actually come true. This book is designed to ensure that you will avoid tight grips and the problems that ensue. Even if your child has been away at college from one to three years already, the window of opportunity for breathing fresh air into family bonds is still open to you.

There are three key aspects of parent–college student relationships in which loosening the parental grip has astoundingly positive effects:

- Coping with strong **emotions**, e.g., missing your child and worrying about her well-being in such a way that you communicate confidence and love, but don't overwhelm her.
- Negotiating how to **stay in touch** via phone calls, visits, E-mails, and learning about what's going on in your child's life, without being intrusive.
- Assisting your child's development and **decision-making**, e.g., choice of major, without interfering.

The overarching goal is to find a new, comfortable balance between connection and separation in your relationship with your child, a process you've been engaging in for many years. You probably used to escort your child to school; later you let her take the bus by herself. Moreover, you've probably gradually increased the hour of your child's curfew over the last few years. In addition, you've probably let your child have sleepovers at friends' houses, and even let her go to sleep-away camp.

As your child has reached each new developmental stage, he has tugged on you for a little more independence. Just when you thought you'd determined the best way to parent, your child went ahead and changed, forcing you to readjust your approach. It's as if your child keeps running on ahead, and by the time you catch up, all out of breath, he takes off again. Parenting is the hardest job you will ever have, and potentially the most rewarding. Now, your child is leaving for college, tugging the hardest he has ever tugged before, and you're wondering, "What will happen to the relationship? How do I parent now?"

In this book, there's a test you can take to find out in which of the three areas of family functioning—emotions, contact, assisting decision-making—you may be having trouble loosening your grip. Then I provide step-by-step guidance on how to readjust the balance between connection and separation so that your relationship with your child is closer than ever and your child can soar. The test and advice are based on interviews I conducted with more than one hundred families experiencing the college transition, as well as statistical analyses of their responses to standardized questionnaires.

A Fun Quiz about Leaving Home:
The Many Hidden Meanings of Laundry

Here's an introduction to what a few of the families had to say about negotiating the college transition. On the surface, the quotes seem to be about laundry, but see if you can identify the underlying relationship themes; in particular, can you detect which family is:

a. Loosening its grip?
b. Holding on too tightly?
c. Experiencing a student overcoming homesickness?
d. Experiencing common parental concern?

The following quotes have a space in which you can fill in the letter for the matching theme:

_____ 1. **A dad:** *I worry about the little silly things, like how he'll wash his clothes. But I know that he can be responsible and that he will do it. But you worry anyway when you're used to taking care of someone.*

_____ 2. **A student:** *Sometimes I call my mom to see what's up, but usually I call because I need something, or because I need her to pick up my dirty laundry. Of course there's talk about what's going on in our lives, not just come and pick up my dirty laundry. I don't think she'd feel she'd lose touch with me because she's still doing things for me, like my laundry. So it's really the same. It's just that I'm not living at the house anymore.*

_____ 3. **A student:** *First semester, I went home every week and did my laundry. Now, I come home every other week.*

_____ 4. **A mom:** *I treat my daughter much more like a grownup. I didn't do her laundry this time she visited. I'm somebody who always has to serve people and for me to not have to do that, and just serve myself is really nice, it's a nice feeling.*

Which quote exemplifies loosening of the parental grip? The mother of quote #4 is enjoying the fact that she has fewer dirty clothes to wash. She's always happy to see her daughter when she comes home and offers her use of the laundry facilities. In fact, she gave her laundry lessons;

laundering is one of the many skills needed for independence, assuming that wash-dry-fold services are not offered for a reasonable cost. There's so much that you will miss with your child out of the house that it's good to let yourself enjoy what you *won't* miss.

Which quote is a red flag for a grip that's too tight? The mom in quote #2 not only washes her child's clothes, but she also picks them up from the dorm and delivers them. The son and mom are in on it together—he calls and she picks up. This mom could make a lot of money offering this service to students. Let's be honest, what parent truly enjoys cleaning somebody else's dirty, smelly socks? Not only are there more satisfying forms of parent-child interaction, but also kids will gain more appreciation for the chores you did for them over the years if you stop doing them. An occasional load, meal, care package, etc., is great, especially when your child is under school stress. Then your child will value your current effort all the more.

Which quote represents a student exhibiting homesickness that improved over time? The #3 student's decrease from freshman to sophomore year in how frequently she went home to do laundry was more an indication of how often she needed to touch base at home for comfort than how much laundry she had to do. Very few people have to do laundry every week. Besides, the cost of gas for her car to travel to and from home probably at least equaled whatever amount she saved on laundering. While your kid cares more about seeing you than she does about doing her laundry, it may be hard for her to admit that she needs you.

Finally, the concerned dad in quote #1 feels what almost all parents feel: worry about how his child will handle responsibilities that used to fall on the parents' shoulders. As long as a parent isn't imagining his child so buried under a pile of laundry that he never makes it to class or that his kid is going to catch an incurable disease from his dirty clothing, then the parent is simply being a parent. As your child proves that he can successfully care for himself, your worries will naturally subside over time.

Most parents find it difficult to have their child leave home. It's how they cope that counts. If you're feeling self-conscious about your strong emotional reaction, then recall these words from the hit television sitcom *3rd*

Rock from the Sun, in which the main characters are aliens who are living on Earth disguised as a human family; their mission is to understand earthlings:

The "father" Dick, whose "son" Harry has just run away from home: *"I wonder how he's doing out there all by himself. You know, if you're a bad father, they leave. If you're a good father, they leave. A parent's love is like a river; no matter how deep or strong its current, it's always flowing toward a sea of separation.*
The "younger son" Tommy: *"Shut up, Dick, you're giving me a Hallmark hernia."*

The focus on loss, no matter how tongue-in-cheek, reminds me of Judith Viorst's best-selling book *Necessary Losses,* about the separation that parents must experience as their children mature. In *Bringing Home the Laundry* I view these separations not as losses, but as necessary changes that actually bring you closer and closer to your child.

To Students

I'm sorry to have to relegate you to a section at the end of each chapter. I'm thrilled that you are reading this book and truly believe that the content can be just as helpful to you as to parents, even the sections addressed to parents. The truth is that parents are much more likely to read this book than are college students, who are usually overwhelmed with assigned reading for classes—you're probably no exception. This book, however, should help decrease any family or school adjustment stress you're feeling and thus save you time by improving your studying efficiency.

Just as parents are told to let go of their college-aged kids, college students are often given the message "Don't go running home to mother," as if they must be completely self-reliant in the alien university world. This is absurd. At college, where everything is new and academic pressures are constant, stress abounds. Odds are that you will freak out from time to time and want Mom and Dad. Rather than being an indication of change resistance, homesickness is a healthy longing for the familiar at a time of insecurity.

This book can help you make the most out of the support that your parents can offer. If your parents are having trouble loosening their grip, then the tips will assist you in establishing a more satisfying degree of independence. You can learn how to effectively communicate your needs to parents without offense, set limits, and be less reactive, all of which, in turn, will alter how your parents view and treat you.

If you're upset that I'm implying that your parents shouldn't do your laundry, it's important to remember that laundry rooms in college dorms are socializing hot spots—a great way to make new friends in your dorm. Also, there's something to be said for privacy; do you really want your parents handling your undies? If you miss your parents and the familiarity of home, there's no harm in going home for a visit, even if your laundry isn't dirty yet.

PART I

Families in Transition

Assisting and Resisting Change

CHAPTER 1

What You Have to Look Forward To

Before we explore the challenges of parenting during this life phase, let me reassure you about all the benefits you can look forward to once you've successfully avoided the potential pitfalls of this period and loosened your grip with the help of this book. Even parents who fear the worst discover pleasant surprises:

Michael, a student: I think my mom felt that we would grow more distant when I moved out because we don't live in the same house anymore. She felt that we would drift apart and just kind of lose touch. And actually, I think the opposite has happened. I think we've gotten close; we know each other better now. I think that was a good thing.

It's natural to assume that a decrease in the quantity of time spent together will result in a decrease in the quality of the time; that physical distance will create emotional distance. In fact, families who loosen their grip find that the opposite is true. Both parents and students reported feeling *closer* to each other than they did during high school. People worry that out of sight means out of mind, but it's really another cliché that applies: Absence makes the heart grow fonder.

Less Conflict

The first principle behind improved relations is that there's less relationship conflict when you're living apart. No longer housemates, you're out of each other's hair. Do you know any two people who live together who never rub each other the wrong way? On top of the everyday squabbles that result from sharing the same space is the added conflict that comes from the parents being the house supervisor. Sound familiar? You come home from work and the stereo is playing loudly; jackets and books are strewn about. You're planning a family dinner, but where is everybody? You hear a voice: Your high school–aged son is talking on the phone instead of studying. "Hey, how's your homework coming along?" you shout.

No response.

"Could you please turn down the stereo and pick up your stuff?"

"Sure Mom, just a minute." A minute becomes a half-hour.

"Dinner's ready."

The family members trickle over to the table, but not your high school kid; he runs out with a wave. "See you later."

"You have to eat. Where are you going?"

"Out for a little while."

"When will you be back?"

"Can't I go anywhere without receiving the third degree?"

The friend on the phone got to hear all the good stuff, while what you heard most was, "Yes, Mom," "Sure, Dad," or worse, "No way!" A lot of monosyllabic dealings. That was your reward for being your child's disciplinarian. Think about your relationships with your boss. Have you ever wondered whether you might enjoy her company more if she wasn't in charge of your salary and job security? I bet the coworkers in your office hang out a lot more with each other than they do with the boss. You know the expression: "It's lonely at the top." Thanks to your child's departure for college, you can still have a say in your child's life and also be that person on the other end of the phone, to whom your kid is enjoying talking:

Jane, a mother: It's been smoother, easier, not as much conflict. When I talk about less conflict, it's really the day-to-day living at home thing.

"Can you please clean your room? Can you please wash the dishes?" No deep-seated conflict, but those petty little conflicts. When she does come home, and has a meal with us, she says, "Oh, let me do the dishes." It's easier.

Valery, Jane's daughter: *We talk a little bit more now. In high school I lived at home, so it was more of a nag thing: "Have you done your homework? Have you done this? Have you done that?" Whereas now, since I come home from my own place, it's "Well, how are things?" We're breaking new boundaries. We even hug once in a while now.*

Kids sitting down for a conversation; children offering to do the dishes before being asked; kids willing to hug you; can this be true? You better believe it, and there's more.

Fewer Struggles for Control

It may be especially hard to believe that tensions ease because the year preceding college is often the tensest period between parents and kids. Kids are itching for independence and scared of it at the same time. They practice being independent by pushing up against parental limits, taking full advantage of whatever leeway they win, and coming back to push for more. A father calls it "the classic teenage high school strain." It's normal for kids to want more freedom at this stage in life, but what makes it extra hard for parents is that this big push for independence comes at a time when the kids are more exposed to alcohol, drugs, and sex. Parental concern rises, while kids' sensitivity to perceiving parental control increases. The high school years can build pressure that leaving home for college can then release:

Susan, a mother: *Nancy has always been extremely independent during her teenage years. And, yet, at the same time, I think she thinks I try to control her too much. But I don't think I do. It has been very important for her to be very independent. Anything that smacks even lightly of control on my part has been seen as that. Since she's been in college I think she's broken away more, and so she's relaxed with me; it doesn't feel like I'm trying to control her.*

So no matter how much your kids may be pushing up against your limits before college begins, all of this can be reversed with leaving home. The trick is to make sure that you're not still playing the role of the room-mate or disciplinarian by always checking up on the student. Now other people are telling your child what to do on a daily basis. Roommates are saying, "Pick up your stuff." Professors are saying, "You need to do your work to get an A in this class." Also, resident advisors in dorms are say-ing, "Keep the noise down." You are freed up to be the good guy, em-pathizing with your child's aggravations.

Since you're no longer your child's house supervisor, relationship conflict can be greatly reduced.

New Conversations

Hearing about What's Going on in Your Child's Life

Having better quality time with your child is more than just the absence of conflict. The time freed up can be filled with new and improved con-versation. Since you're no longer the daily overseer, your kids can feel more comfortable sharing personal information that they may have previ-ously kept to themselves:

Jimmy, a student: In high school, my father and I didn't really talk. It was mostly formal talk, like, "Hi, how are you doing? How is work? How is school?" I find that since I've started college, we could talk less tensely; it's not a forced conversation. I can talk to him on a more friendly level and we talk about adult things, like, what I'm going to do when I get a job, and what's going on in college, or with women, or in the fraternity. He tells me about how some of his buddies nearly flunked out of school. He can empathize with all that stuff because the same thing happened to him.

Your child can be more open with you because he knows that you won't be there at college to monitor every little detail as the drama continues to unfold. Jimmy's dad was able to draw upon his own past experience to counsel his son, but don't worry if you don't have similar experiences to draw from. As long as you avoid coming across as judgmental and focus on being a good sounding board, you'll make a great parental consultant.

Your Child Asking You for Advice

College students not only may talk more openly about their lives, but also may ask parents more directly for advice, and even agree with the advice—quite a different picture from the typical high school years. As one student said, "I go to my parents for advice and help when I need it, but they aren't there to tell me what to do anymore. I like the change."

High school is a time when kids are struggling within themselves to forge an identity of their own. They fear being swallowed up by the strong personality of others in the household, namely their parents. The identity kids take on is, more often than not, quite similar to that of their parents. Nonetheless, they need to establish themselves as separate individuals by disagreeing with parents' views and trying to work out problems on their own. Once the kids have proven that they're independent people by living on their own, then they can feel freer to agree with parents and listen to their guidance.

Because college students often feel more similar to parents in terms of values than they do to many of their classmates, touching base with home can now be a source of comfort. It's like you—the parent—are a boxer waiting in the ring with your gloves on ready to fight when challenged. But instead of entering the ring, your opponent—your child—tells you to take the gloves off and go for a walk together.

The physical distance of being out of the house may free your child up to share more personal information and ask for advice.

Time Spent Together Is Appreciated

Family conversation at this phase in life also becomes more meaningful because time together is more precious:

Tamari, a student: I think that you appreciate each other a lot more when you're not living in the same house. It's inevitable that if somebody's always

*there for you, you take it for granted. I'm closer to my parents now than I
was before, and I realize I didn't appreciate them as much as I do now. I've
now figured out that they're pretty neat people. I like to talk to them. I don't
seem them as much, and the time I spend with them I value more than I used
to. So, I guess I spend more quality time with them. We talk less about the
trivial, day-to-day things, and more about the important stuff.*

In high school, a passing in the kitchen might have gone something
like this:
"Hey Tina, how was your day?"
"Fine, Dad."
"How was school?"
"Same old, same old."
"And that test?"
"Hard. Really hard. But at least it's over. Well, got to go call Kelly about
the homework. See you later."
In college, there are no accidental passings in the kitchen; parents and
students have to make an effort to track each other down. Students are
happy to have a captive parental audience to talk to about classes, professors' personalities, challenges of upcoming exams, roommate troubles
(assuming the roommate is out of earshot), and, if you're lucky, budding
romances. Of course all of this isn't automatic. Parents have to make sure
not to crowd students too much.

More Conversations about the World

So what is your child doing with all of her time? She's exploring new
worlds in and out of class. Maybe she's studying new exciting topics—like
psychology or economics. Perhaps she's relating what she learns to what
she sees around her: the group psychology behind library behavior during
finals; the supply and demand principle behind the climbing prices of rock
concert tickets. Possibly she's joined special interest clubs and made friends
with students from other parts of the country or the world. She pays attention to news now; her university made headlines by changing its affir-
mative action policies, or there's a military coup in her friend's home
country. She's starting to think more seriously about a major, a career, and

what it's like to be part of the workforce. Maybe she holds down a part-time job.

You, the parent, have been in the working world and paying attention to the news for quite some time. Now, your child's world is expanding to include the universe you've inhabited for years. Perhaps she's discovering ones that are new to you. As your child's realm expands, there's an opportunity for your relationship to expand as well:

Brenda, a mother: *We were just really pleased with the way that Keith turned out. For example, rather than him just listening to my opinions, I ask his opinion on political issues because he's studying them at school. We have discussions, intriguing conversations, and political debates. As a result, the relationship actually gets a lot better, because it seems to me there's more of him that's going to be relating back to me and everyone else. It's going to be more varied and different, and I think it's nice when it's not the same.*

During the high school years it was harder to have purely intellectual debates because your child was more suspicious that you were trying to influence his behavior, as if the real struggle was over how he would lead his life, not over ideas. College affords you new conversational opportunities as long as you avoid using intellectual discussion to persuade him of a "right way," or feeling overly threatened to your child's intellectual exploration in new directions.

An added benefit to stimulating conversations is that you get more bang for your college buck. Your kid is the recipient of the most up-to-date research and information, and therefore, probably has interesting facts to relate. Just think of what a kick it is for your child to be able to impart knowledge to you. It's incredibly empowering and does wonders for his self-esteem.

Your child's intellectual expansion can enrich your family conversations.

Increased Mutual Respect

New conversations about the world are just one of the reasons that parents and their college-aged children hold each other in greater mutual esteem. Parents who have successfully launched their children into college talk about how proud they are to see their kids functioning on their own. Instead of seeing the child who left her dirty clothes around the house, didn't do the dishes, and stayed out beyond curfew, you can see the child who lives on her own and attends college:

Stanley, a father: I see my son as much more of an adult than I did when he was in our house. He's much more independent and makes his own decisions. Each year he continues to be more adult and we continue to treat him as more of an independent adult. He's moved from boyhood to manhood. I see my relationship with my son getting better. A lot of it has to do with my being comfortable with his ability to cope. I had some doubts as to whether he could continue his rambunctious life and still work hard and get good grades. But he did it, and he's doing well, and I think he's learning in the process.

Even if your child isn't earning the best possible grades or handling finances responsibly, there's almost always something to be proud of, like the fact that he manages to eat, sleep, wear clean clothes, and get to class. Parental respect and pride are important. As a parent you need to pat yourself on the back for a job well done, and your child needs to know that you believe in him. How parents view students carries a lot of weight. You may think that your child's professors' feedback and grades have more impact on your child than your evaluation, but the opposite is true. For all of his life, your child has been looking to you for approval, and that hasn't changed. Kids are too close to their own maturation process to take account of their gains; they need parents to reflect their growth back to them:

Charlene, a student: My parents think that I've changed a lot, become more mature and more responsible. They always think that every time they see me I look older and I act more maturely. But since I live by myself every day, I don't see that.

Making sure that your child sees a positive reflection of herself when she looks into your eyes will increase the warmth in your relationship, and go a long way in contributing to your child's actual success. Even if you and your child got into a cycle of mistrust during high school, your opportunity to express confidence in your child is wide open at this new stage.

While seeing your child as more and more of an adult is beneficial, it is possible to take this tendency to a harmful extreme. Some parents find it tempting to have their grown child as their best friend, their main confidant in times of trouble. This elevation of child to peer can pollute the relationship, and hinder the student's adjustment to college.

Troubled Relationships Improve

Now is the time that really troubled parent-child relationships have a window of opportunity to improve. One of the main reasons that this is so is that the increased mutual respect and physical distance enable each person to see the other's perspective in ways they were blinded to before:

Janelle, a student whose family is still living back home overseas:
When I lived at home, I thought my mother was the worst person in the world. Now that I'm away from home, I don't hate her as much, because when she calls me up and nags me, I'm more tolerant and I can see more of how that comes from her excessive care for us, rather than me attributing that to her bad character.

Jordan, a student whose father is mentally ill and violent: My mom *suddenly realized that things are not okay with me and how hard it was for me being at home. She's much nicer to me now.*

When parents and students gain new perspectives on family relationships, old tensions are eased.

Sibling relationships can also go from tense to harmonious:

Brenda, a mother: My son Keith and his sister are very competitive. Their *personalities are very alike, so they used to fight a lot when they were in high* *school, but they've gotten real close since he's been away. They do a lot of the outdoor backpacking and those sorts of things together. And that bridged some of the conflicts they had. Their relationship has improved 100 percent. The sibling rivalry that was there as they were growing up isn't there anymore.*

When a child leaves for college, the siblings are no longer competing on the same playing field. The move is especially helpful when the two siblings were attending the same high school. The younger sibling now has a chance to make his own path and can play the role of keeping the older sibling informed about the home activities, while the older sibling can introduce the younger sibling to the adult college world.

Parents and students also report having an all-around good time together. Parents are happy that their kid is less embarrassed to be seen with the family in public. Makes sense—college is proof enough of one's independence. Students report that parents often seem in better spirits than usual. Sure they are. They're pleased as can be that they're seeing their kid and want the time to be enjoyable.

Benefits to Your Personal Life

This new phase can also benefit your personal life. If you loosen your grip on your child, a good marriage gets better, a troubled marriage can possibly be restored, and more energy can be focused on fulfilling career dreams.

Are you currently married? If so, then you're probably wondering, "What will happen to my marriage with the kids growing up and leaving the house?" Much of the joy and pain you and your spouse shared together for at least the past seventeen years were kid related. Perhaps against all odds you were able to stay fully acquainted with each other as romantic partners separate from being Mom and Dad. More likely, you lost each other somewhat along the way and will be facing a reunion of sorts. Emotions range from nervous excitement to fear of what the future together will hold:

Francesca, a mom: When you spend twenty-two years wrapped up in your kids, and all of a sudden your nest is empty, there has to be a moment that you say, "My god! I don't know if my husband and I are gonna like each other." I went through that. I had REAL mixed emotions about it. I didn't think our marriage would fall apart, but I wondered how much work it was gonna take, you know, to get to know each other, because we did sacrifice a lot for our kids.

If you're worried that your marriage will fall apart, there's good news. The widespread belief that half, if not more, of all marriages end in divorce is based on faulty statistical analyses. When one compares the number of people divorcing in a year to the number of people who are already married, then you get a more comforting figure; somewhere between 18 and 22 percent of all marriages are dissolved. Are you already breathing a little sigh of relief? There's more: The average age at which people experience their first marital breakup is in their early- to mid-thirties—certainly not the age at which their kids are leaving for college. Research found that the biggest dip in marital satisfaction comes right after the kids are born and continues when they are young. So it seems like the odds are in your favor that if your union hasn't become defunct already, in all likelihood, it won't. Also, if you've already experienced the marital satisfaction dip, then it can only get better from here. In fact, this is what most couples found:

Francesca, the mother who spoke of her fears: My husband David and I traveled. We had an absolute ball. And we ENJOYED each other's company. It was probably the best vacation I have EVER had in my life; it was so free. We could have sex whenever we wanted to, we could get up whenever we wanted to. I never worried about eating or food with David. With my kids, you know, there were all these meals, and there were all these THINGS you had to be doing. We had a ball. Then back at home, we started rediscovering common interests other than the children.

Parents' marital relationships tend to improve when their child leaves for college.

Even for very troubled marriages, there can be a little fresh air breathed into the bond. In the Kreiger family, the father had been having a secretive extramarital affair that has included the birth of a baby, and yet both partners experienced marital benefits to the empty nest:

Marcus, the father: The attitude changed in the relationship. My wife made a lot of suggestions which she hadn't made to me for years about, well, let's go take a trip to this place, let's go do this, let's do that. I think it'll be a good thing.

There's also great potential for your sex life to improve. Women reach their sexual peak in their late twenties to early thirties and stay there through age sixty. Men may reach their sexual peak in their twenties and fall downward, but the availability of Viagra and other medical aids help them keep pace with their mates. There's no reason that your sex life can't be better than ever before.

In addition to an increase in the positive, there also tends to be a decrease in some negative aspects of the relationship:

Anita, a mom: When you don't have the kids around there aren't as many hassles between the couple, like who's gonna do what and all that. It's just a much more casual lifestyle than when they were children; some of the problems are gone.

With fewer immediate parenting challenges, there are fewer incidents of parental head butting. No matter how compatible you and your spouse might be, you rarely agree on every parenting issue. You also have more time to resolve whatever negative conflict exists between you two.

You don't need to be left with an empty nest for the departure to have benefits. Sometimes marital conflict has come to revolve around a particular child; so when that child leaves, peace is restored:

Rebecca, a student: I get along so much better with my mother than my father, and I can see that it would definitely ease their relationship with me not living at home. My father and I disagree on almost everything; my mom often takes my side, and I know that that causes a lot of friction between her and my dad.

Even when parents are divorced or separated, a child's departure can make the relationship more amicable:

Tom, a student: My parents, who are divorced, speak more to each other and are on better terms because I'm not there to relay messages back and forth about certain issues, like money situations.

Of course, there are families in which the child's departure presents a real threat to the marriage:

Hector, a father: Having the kids here is cement for the marriage. My wife and I were both dealing with children, but when the children go away, there are fewer things that we have in common because some of the key things that we did together aren't there anymore. We don't have those decisions that we have to team up on, so it leaves us with our own things to do and not so many joint things to do.

Rather than being a time to split apart, your child's departure can afford you the perfect opportunity to tackle your marital differences and troubles head-on. A dose of couples therapy or even just a long vacation alone together could be just what you need to get your marriage back on track.

All of these wonderful changes in family relationships and your personal life are in your grasp. They're not magic, and they're not automatic, but they are obtainable with a little conscious effort. Families in which the college student reluctantly remained at home reported that their relationships either stayed the same or got worse when college began. In families where the kids left home but parents maintained a tight hold, parents and students reported few gains, and new troubles. Yet, when parents were able to ease their anxiety and loosen their grips, the benefits flowed. You too can avoid parenting pitfalls and reap the benefits of this period.

To Students

All these opportunities to become closer to your parents and gain their support are open to you. Even if parents are giving you flack for how you're handling your life, there's probably hidden pride in there and we'll find it. Don't worry, you won't have to hug your parents all the time or divulge intimate secrets to enjoy their company more. You can just be you.

CHAPTER 2

_____

_____

_____

Change Assisters and Change Resisters

After reading the last chapter, you might be asking yourself, "Can all of these relationship benefits really flow from loosening my grip on my child?" The answer is yes. This chapter covers loosening your grip in concrete parenting terms.

Being a Secure Base for Your Child

Loosening your grip without letting go means that you're being a **secure base** for your child; the security you provide enables her to explore the world and take risks. Remember when your child first learned to walk and would wander away from you for a short distance to examine a toy? She would be totally engrossed in her new activity, until suddenly, she'd break her concentration to look at you. You'd smile at her and she'd resume her exploration. Then suddenly, she'd break her concentration again to bring you a toy. Why didn't she just keep playing, oblivious to all around her? Why did she periodically need to make contact with you? For all her boldness in exploring the universe around her, she was nervous as well. Newness can be overwhelming. To calm her anxiety, she would touch base with you—her secure base.

The comfort of your nurturing presence allowed her to examine the unfamiliar. As the circle of her exploration became wider and wider, as her universe expanded to encompass school, activities, and many new people, she still needed to touch base with you, but the touching base took on different forms. Instead of looking to you for a reassuring glance, she would come home from school and tell you about her day. Instead of bringing you a toy, she would introduce you to her friends.

Upon arriving at college, the size of your child's world multiplied by one hundred within a matter of minutes: new people, new home, new food, new academics, new responsibilities, everything new down to the toilet paper. Sure, your child is older now, and better prepared to handle the world. But this amount of novelty is tremendous; she needs you to be her secure base as much as ever before. Now, instead of offering a reassuring glance, you're available by telephone when your child needs to talk. Instead of accepting a toy, you provide a healthy meal and a warm bed whenever she appears at the door:

Kathleen, a mom: *Kids in college are still young kids, and they still want support, and they still want homemade cookies, and they still want cards in their mailbox; they still need all those things. But, I didn't know that before she left—I'm happy to know that my child still needs me.*

As a secure base for a college-aged child, you are a support system waiting in the wings, ready to be tapped anytime your child shows signs of needing help and comfort:

Richard, a dad: *I think that part of the job of being the parent is to get them out and let them do what they need to do. My wife and I are a support system that he's comfortable using. How he generates that support system is up to him. So, we're comfortable with that.*

Surrendering to Your Child's Rhythm

Being a support system for your child, like most significant jobs in life, is easier said than done. A writer cited in the *New York Times*, Marc Parent, described the challenge well:

Hardly anyone is cut out for this kind of servitude. The biggest thing about parenting is surrender. You have to surrender to the rhythm of the child. It's like when you break a horse—every new parent has to be broken by their newborn.

This process of "surrendering to your child's rhythm" started during pregnancy and still continues to this day. You've spent years trying to understand and accommodate what he needs. As your child has changed over the years, so too has the way he's communicated his needs. When he was an infant, a sputtering cry might have meant he was tired, while a wailing one meant he was hungry. Now, a week without a call home might indicate that he's happily settled into school, while a surprise visit home at midnight might signify that he's having trouble adapting. After studying your child for so long, trying to decode the language of his body, the tone of his voice, and the meaning behind his actions, you are an expert in what your child needs—even if you feel clueless, you aren't. You could write a dissertation entitled *My Child* and earn your Ph.D. in *The Study of My Child.*

The key to being a good secure base is taking the cues from your child.

Of course, some kids are easier to read than others and some parents have better preparation for being secure bases than others. There's a lot that goes into being able to interpret a child's cues and respond appropriately. Don't worry—you don't have to be a mind-reading psychic. You can be a secure-base parent through trial and error, as long as you remain sensitive to deciphering cause and effect, and flexible enough to keep trying out new strategies. Taking a back seat while having to be alert and on call may sound like a thankless job, especially since you rarely receive direct gratitude when you perform the role well, and yet get a lot of flack when you slip up. Thus, being a secure base for your child is the most important position you will ever hold in your life.

The Three-Generational Effect

Meet the Evans family, who talk about what it's like to be a secure base for your college-aged child day in and day out. As you read, listen for the first clue as to what preparation the Evanses received that facilitated their ability to respond to their child's cues:

Kathleen, the mother: For being a parent I look back to my own experience. When I was Pamela's age, my mother was rather clingy, that's a mild way of putting it. When I went away to school, I had to call home, and I had to come home. So when my daughter Pamela went to college, I was determined to let her make those decisions herself. So I never said, "Why haven't you come home? Are you going to come home next weekend?" That was her decision all year, when to come home. If there was some kind of particular event going on, I would let her know about it, but it was always her decision. I didn't let my-self get upset if she thought she couldn't come home that weekend. It turned out she came home far more than I would have expected. She called far more than I would have expected her to call. It worked out fine. But I was very much determined not to make her do things because it was my need. I let her do what she needed to do and it worked out fine for both of us.

The more Kathleen was able to operate according to her child's needs for contact, as opposed to her own, the more her daughter surprised her mother by initiating contact. How did Kathleen learn to be sensitive to her daughter's cues? She distinctly recalls how restricted she felt when her own mother took control of how and when they stayed in touch. Rather than push this memory way back into her unconscious, she purposefully kept it at the forefront of her conscious mind, making it a top-priority mission that she parent her college-aged daughter the exact opposite way of how her own mother parented her. Kathleen enlisted her mother as an anti-role model. This is a **three-generational effect.** Of course it's easier if you are fortunate enough to want to emulate the way your parents handled your home leaving. Yet, only a few people have been blessed with such perfect role models.

Think about how your parent(s) handled your becoming an adult who lived independently and attended college. Did they loosen their grips, hold on too tightly, or push you away? Were you happy with how they handled the transition? Did they treat you too much like a child or maybe even too much like an adult? Now that you're the parent, do you want to follow your parents' approach with your own child upon the start of college? If not, how determined are you to take a different approach?

The biggest stumbling block to utilizing your parents as anti-role models is guilt that you are betraying them. Comfort your conscience with the thought that your parents probably did the best they could under the circumstances, but you owe it to them, to your child, and to yourself to do the best you can under your current circumstances. Take pride in taking control of the three-generational cycle and creating a new path for future generations. Think of yourself as Luke Skywalker in *Star Wars* fighting a powerful but invisible force—you can't see it, but you can feel its presence.

Think about how your own parents approached parenting you when you embarked on adulthood. How is this affecting the grip you have on your young adult child?

Life Cycle Effects

Back to the Evanses. Just because these parents were able to act according to their child's needs doesn't mean that it was easy for them to override their own needs. Often, parents who are able to loosen their grips still find it to be an internal struggle. Kathleen said that she had to prevent herself from picking up the phone and from becoming upset if her daughter didn't visit. These urges were extra strong because Pamela Evans is one of two kids in the family; she has a twin sister who left home at exactly the same time. When you read what they have to say about how emotional the experience was for them, look for two more clues as to how they were able to adjust to the departure:

Thomas: A day or two after both kids left, my wife and I were sitting in the kitchen talking about the kids and all of a sudden, I realized that everything that I said was in the past tense and it made me extremely sad. We were crying. And two or three days later, we were fine. I think that it's appropriate for them to grow up and go away.

Kathleen: *My husband and I have talked about it, and we feel really ambivalent, both sad and glad at the same time; we acknowledge both of those so it's okay. There were times when we were very lonely and missed them both very much and times when it was really very nice to have our private home back again, to not have kids around, and to have quiet in the house again. Usually people do that gradually, because they have one older and one younger; we did it all at once.*

The Evanses had a house full of kids one day, and an empty nest the next. Even though these parents enjoy each other's company, they still suffered a sense of loneliness. Kids fill up your life in a different way than spouses do: the joy of watching them mature, the responsibility felt for their well-being, and the dynamism that they bring into the family as they grow. When your child departs, leaving you with either an empty nest or just an emptier nest, you will feel that the household has changed.

What is the second clue as to why the Evanses are able to be good secure bases? They can think of the positive aspects of their twins' departure as well as the negative—be glad as well as sad. The third clue? What helped the Evanses be so open and productive with their emotions is that both parents could openly acknowledge feelings of ambivalence and vulnerability in the other's company. Being sad became a shared experience between the parents that gave each other the message that it's normal to feel this way and reaffirmed their bond. This level of spousal closeness isn't always easy to achieve, especially when parents are excited, but nervous about what it's going to be like having more time alone with each other. Let us not forget that many of you reading this book are single parents or in an unhappy marriage. Coping with emotional upheaval and being a secure base for your child is certainly attainable—just give yourself credit for facing the extra challenge of adjusting without the support of a spouse.

The fact that the Evanses turned to their marital relationship, which had strengthened through years of parenting as a team, to pull through their children's leaving home is a positive **life cycle effect.** You and your child have been traveling through your own individual, yet intersecting, life paths. When your first child came into the world, she turned you into a parent. Now that your child is beginning college, embarking on adult professional and romantic paths, you have more time to attend to your own romantic and professional lives.

This may feel like a mid-life phase, in which you are reevaluating your own choices in these areas. Your child asks himself, "Who am I? What do I want from a mate? What do I want to do with my life?" You may be asking yourself, "Have I become who I wanted to become? Is there something more that I want from a mate? Does my career path make me happy?" This can be a very exciting, yet challenging time for everybody. You might even find yourself being a little envious of the opportunities that lie ahead for your child. This is normal, but it's also important to reassure yourself that this can be the start of a new exploratory phase for you, too.

Parents who are looking forward to spending more time with a spouse or getting more deeply involved in a profession will have a smoother adjustment period. It's easier to be a secure base for your child when you feel secure in your own life and have your own supports.

Are there any major disappointments in your life? High expectations you had for a marriage that fell short? Dreams you had for a career that never materialized? Unfulfilled desire you had to mend relations with your own parents and siblings? Dashed hopes you had for financial comfort, less pressure, better health, or more lighthearted laughter? Odds are that you have experienced some degree of disappointment, but maybe some pleasant surprises as well. The question is, on balance, do you feel like you have any gaping holes in your life? If the answer isn't immediately clear, think about what happens when you watch a movie or a television show; which characters do you envy most? Those who have the passionate love affairs, those who have the solid marriages, those who have exciting careers, those who have a loving extended family, or those with a close-knit group of friends?

Accepting your own disappointments is the first step in healing them. Remember, thinking about disappointments won't make them worse; confronting them can only make them better. For the purpose of parenting your college-aged child, you don't have to fill in these gaps, but be aware that they're there; tell yourself that having your child leave home is especially difficult for you because you feel there's something missing in your life. Give yourself a break.

Rather than signal an end to your parenting career, your child leaving home marks a new parenting phase and also frees up some of your time to pursue other activities, including spending more time with a spouse, getting more involved in your job, or switching careers. Careers that once seemed challenging may have become old hat and boring. Marriages that revolved around the day-to-day demanding tasks of raising kids in the home now have a chance to bloom in new ways.

Think about how fulfilled you feel in your own life right now. How is this affecting the grip you have on your young adult child?

The Evanses had the benefit of other positive life cycle effects in addition to a happy marriage. They were both highly satisfied with their jobs at the same children's book publishing company and had a support system of friends who were going through the same family life cycle phase. Pamela summed up the situation well:

I felt comfortable about the process of leaving home and I felt that my parents adjusted to it. It took a little while, but we are all quite happy about it now. Right now, my parents miss me but it doesn't leave a gaping hole in their lives. I was happy that they were willing to let me go and let me develop on my own. I miss them, but I was happy to start stretching my wings.

The key phrase here is that Pamela's departure did not leave a "gaping hole" in her parents' lives. Pamela, in turn, came to enjoy college life, make close friends, and achieve among the highest grade point averages of any student participating in the study. Note how Pamela said "stretch her wings," not "fly away." The image of stretching her wings is one of continuing her exploration of the world while still being close to the nest.

With the Evanses, it sounds like the *Brady Bunch*'s Cindy and Bobby are both leaving for college. But let's imagine the Bunkers in *All in the Family* when their only child, Gloria, is departing for university—that would be a different story. There was a good deal of shouting in the Bunker household, the marriage was often tense, Archie always complained about his job, and they had a sprinkling of friends. Is it any wonder that American television viewers identified more with the Bunkers than they did with the Brady clan? Since we don't know how difficult it was for the Bunkers when their daughter Gloria left home for college, let's meet a real family, the Warrens.

Secure Base Reversal

The Warrens live only a twenty-minute car ride from where their only child, Sam, is living on his college campus. Just like the Evanses, the Warrens are very sad to be left with an empty nest, and have a solid marriage and a warm and loving relationship with their child. But unlike the Evanses, Marshall Warren was emotionally devastated by his son's departure:

Marshall, the father: I was very sad that Sam's departure had come to pass. I feel better about it now, but it did trigger a depression, my mid-life crisis, and my emptiness syndrome—it really did. It was almost like a death or a divorce, a sudden separation; it's an extreme change in your life, especially in our life when you have an only child leaving. You are all living together twenty-four hours a day and then all of a sudden one person is gone for extended periods of time. That's a real interruption to normal routine and can affect people emotionally. I loved being a father and got so much satisfaction from it, that when my son left, the balance in my life really changed a lot . . . his leaving left a big hole.

Marshall fell into a clinical depression: decreased appetite and energy level, tearfulness, low self-esteem—the whole set of symptoms. Compare how Pamela mentioned that her departure did not leave a gaping hole in her parents' lives, but how Marshall stated that his son's departure did. The phrase "big hole" clues us into the fact that a life cycle effect is playing a role; both Sam and his father talked about a career gap as being the cause. Marshall had been using his Ph.D. in biochemistry to run a pharmaceuticals company, but then switched to stockbrokering in order to put his son through private high school:

Marshall: When Sam left, I was suddenly faced with things that I have been putting off; his leaving was a trigger, because I don't actually need more of Sam than I already have. It's how I used Sam, not manipulating him as a person, but what he represented in my life. When he moved out, that triggered an awareness that took time, several months; I realized, "Hey, I've got to do something with my life that makes it better." Let's say if he didn't have to go off to college, I don't think that I would have gone into a depression. It's very hard to put into words that phenomenon of how, psychologically, I used the cover of fathering to give myself a kind of satisfaction that I don't get any-more—not to say that I don't get a lot of satisfaction being with Sam any-more—but I need something more in my life now.

We can hear clearly how hard this transition was for Marshall. What kind of effect did this have on his relationship with his son? Sam and his dad spoke on the phone *at least* once every day. Marshall continued the role he had established during the high school years as Sam's secretary: buying Sam's books and organizing his academic life. Similarly, Sam came home regularly to actually help his parents with chores around the house: Sam said, "I help with housework and stuff, that takes some of the burden off of my parents."

Most kids barely take the time to tidy up their own rooms, let alone help their parents out when they return for visits. You may be thinking, "I see no problem here. What lucky parents. I wish that my child would come home to help with chores." But there were problems. Sam was putting so much emotional and physical energy into trying to assuage his father's distress that his adjustment at school suffered. This extremely articulate boy who wanted to be a state senator was earning near failing grades in college; in high school he had earned the second top grade point average in his class. The very warm father-son relationship was starting to chill a little, and the dad was focusing more on his son's departure than on improving his professional situation.

The Warrens are experiencing what I call a **secure base reversal.** Of course, parents draw comfort and solace from their relationships with their children, but when a child becomes the filler for life's holes, trouble brews. Marshall described it perfectly when he said, "that phenomenon of how, psychologically, I used the cover of fathering to give myself a kind of satisfaction that I don't get anymore." By keeping the relationship as similar as could be to how it was in high school, staleness set in—plus Dad was too depressed to enjoy the time he did spend with his son.

A secure base reversal occurs when a child becomes a parent's primary source of comfort and meaning, covering up a hole in the parent's life.

Marshall didn't even know that he was clinically depressed until he went to see a therapist who helped him identify the symptom pattern and the underlying source of his unhappiness. As he shifted the focus in therapy from his son leaving to dealing with his own career dissatisfaction, the depression lifted. As his depression lifted, his son's grades lifted as well, back up to his high school level of excellence. I wouldn't be surprised if Sam were elected senator some day. Sam and his dad also found their relationship strengthening—it was no longer based on taking out the garbage and washing the dishes together, but on attending sporting events and discussing world politics.

Change Resistance, Assistance, and Desistance

Because he was scared of losing the type of closeness that he and his son had shared during the high school period, Marshall tried to maintain the father-son relationship just as it had been. This process of trying to prevent relationship changes in the face of a life cycle transition is what I call **change resistance.** It usually leads to increased emotional distance within the family, just the opposite effect of what the parent hopes to achieve.

We know that if you let parent-child relationship changes occur naturally to accommodate the new phase, then you'll be pleasantly surprised by how wonderful the changes can be. Facilitating the evolution that accompanies the college transition is what I call **change assistance;** this is what Kathleen and Thomas Evans did.

A third possibility is that if family life is fraught with strife, parents are eager for their children to leave the house. As a result, the family focuses more on celebrating the decreased daily conflict than on rebuilding the relationship with their child; this is **change desistance.**

If you have more than one child, you might find that you're a change resister with one, and an assister with another; siblings play different roles in their parents' lives.

> When parents facilitate the natural relationship changes that flow from the college transition, they are *assisting change*. When a parent tries to prevent the relationship changes, then they are *resisting change*. When parents pay more attention to the relief from conflict that the departure brings than to how the relationship will continue, then they are *change desisters*.

Combating Change Resistance

Marshall's depression had been so disruptive to his life that he was compelled to seek professional help. With the help of a therapist he tackled the source of his change resistance head-on—he mourned the loss of his original career dream and went on to search for a new one. To fight change resistance at the source—large life issues—parents might seek career counseling, demand a promotion, change jobs, attend couples therapy, or seek supportive grief counseling over a deceased loved one.

Another effective way to combat change resistance is to focus on the specific behaviors and thoughts that constitute a tight grip, and then learn ways to loosen up. Even though there are many different causes of parental change resistance, there is a common set of emotions, expectations, and actions that these parents share, and the Change Resistance Test in the next chapter taps into this. By taking the test you can identify the exact ways in which you are resisting and assisting change and then read on to learn change-assisting tips.

To Students

1. A first step in claiming your parents as a secure base is for you to contemplate where their reactions to your home leaving are coming from—not to excuse them, but so that you can take their parenting approach less person-

ally. To gain a less emotionally charged perspective, consider your parents as individuals with a history (three-generational effect) and a present life (life cycle effects).

2. What were the circumstances under which your parents left home for the first time? How did their parents react? Supportive, resistant, indifferent? Any stories from this period? How did your parents feel about how their parents handled their departures? Odds are that you don't know the answers to these questions. Why not ask your parents about their leaving home? If they attended college, you can couch your inquiry in terms of the entire transition, asking about school social life and academics, as well as their parents' reactions.

3. The next task is to determine how your parents are coping in the here and now. Are there any gaping holes in their lives? Are they happy in their jobs? Did they have a passion that went unexplored? Is their marriage a happy one? Or are your parents happily single, or unhappily so? For these questions you don't need to interview your parents. After living with them for eighteen years, you have a sense of how they feel, even if they're not people who emote about the bad day at work or fight with each other in the living room.

4. What's important for you to keep in mind is that no matter what you do—go far away to school or stay close by, visit infrequently or visit all the time—the holes in your parents' lives will still be there. The best thing you can do for yourself and the family is to go on with your life according to your plan and be happy. Sometimes parents have to sink a little lower, as Marshall did into his depression, to realize that they need help and then obtain assistance, so that they can climb high into happiness.

5. Understanding where your parents are coming from can help you see them as the fallible humans that they are. Empathy does not mean acceptance; you still need to fight for having your parents assist the necessary changes that go along with starting college and the road to adulthood. This is where the Change Resistance Test comes in; take the test for all of your parental figures and determine where they are succeeding in assisting change and where they fall short. Then read on to learn what you can do about it.

PART II

The Change Resistance Test

CHAPTER 3

Taking and Scoring the Change Resistance Test

Now is your chance to find out whether your own grip is too tight, or too loose, or just right. Taking the Change Resistance Test, which will tap into your emotional and behavioral reaction to your child moving out, will enable you to determine in what ways you're facilitating positive changes in your relationship with your child, and in what ways you may be hindering those beneficial developments.

The test assesses the three main areas of parent-child interaction: emotions, contact, and decision-making. You may find that you assist change easily in one area, while another may be more of a struggle. You may also find that accepting the relationship changes that this phase of life imposes is difficult for you across the board. Take comfort in the fact that you are not alone; the majority of the parents interviewed found the college transition difficult to traverse. If accepting your child leaving were easy, then our culture wouldn't have coined the term "letting go" in the first place, and there wouldn't be a whole book about "loosening your grip."

If you discover that your tendency is to resist change, don't chastise yourself—just feel motivated to learn how to assist change, knowing that the natural benefits will follow. Your goal is to be the securest possible base for your child. Following the test is a description of what it means to assist and resist change in each area of family interaction. You can trust that I won't leave you hanging—subsequent chapters provide step-by-step advice on how to achieve your parenting goals.

When taking the test, be completely honest with yourself. You are the only person who will see your responses. Sometimes it's hard to admit uncomfortable feelings, even to oneself. Moreover, this is an important enough transition in the lives of you and your child that it's worth confronting him. Denial of change resistance greatly compounds its negative effects. Accepting that your grip may be a little too tight is the first step in loosening it.

The questionnaire is written as if your child has already left home for school. If your child hasn't started college yet or is living at home and commuting to school, then interpret the test to mean, "When my child leaves home," or "If my child were to leave home," respectively.

Write your answers to the questions on the answer sheet—as opposed to the test itself—so that after you've worked to loosen your grip, you can take the test again six months from now and not be influenced by your initial responses. It's always nice to take stock of the fruits of your efforts. To feel as comfortable as possible when taking the test, create circumstances that maximize confidentiality: Take the test far away from all family members (behind a closed, maybe even locked, door), and keep the book in a private place.

Grab a pencil, close the door, and let's go to the test on page 43.

To Students

Take the Change Resistance Test separately for each parent. Please adapt the test to the particular configuration of your family, be it a mom and dad, one parent, two mothers, a stepparent, or a grandparent.

When answering the questions, you will be imagining how your parents think and feel. Although you may feel inadequately prepared to answer for another family member, let me assure you, people don't live in the same house together for more than seventeen years without being highly attuned to what goes on in each other's minds. Even a best guess will be well informed; whatever is too conflicted for the brain to confront, intuition knows. Gut feelings rarely lie, as long as denial doesn't run deep.

It's important that you answer the questions as honestly as you possibly can. Be assured that by doing so you're not betraying your parents. Taking an honest look at your family will ultimately help everybody adjust better to your departure. As we all know, ignoring bad feelings doesn't make them go away. If it did, therapists would be out of business.

The Change Resistance Test

1.

1	2	3	4	5	6	7
I urged my child to be close to home.			I let my child choose college distance.			I wanted my child to be far from home.

2.

1	2	3	4	5	6	7
I'm very sad about my child leaving home.			I'm pleased and sad about my child leaving home.			I'm very happy about my child leaving home.

3.

1	2	3	4	5	6	7
I'm upset if my child doesn't call or visit often.			I understand if my child doesn't call or visit often.			I don't care if my child calls or visits.

4.

1	2	3	4	5	6	7
I wanted my child to live at home.			I let my child choose where to live.			I didn't allow my child to live at home.

5.

1	2	3	4	5	6	7
I'm very concerned for my child's well-being.			I'm somewhat concerned, but trust my child to take care.			I'm not concerned for my child.

6.

1	2	3	4	5	6	7
I feel that the amount of phone calls, E-mails, and visits is much too little.			I feel that the amount of contact is just right.			I feel that the amount of contact is too much.

please turn page

7. ←———————————————————————————→

1	2	3	4	5	6	7
I wish that my child were more dependent on me financially.			I'm happy with how financially dependent my child is.			I wish that my child were less financially dependent.

8. ←———————————————————————————→

1	2	3	4	5	6	7
I fear that my relationship with my child will greatly weaken with my child leaving home.			I am confident that my relationship with my child will continue and be strong.			I don't think about how the relationship will continue with my child leaving home.

9. ←———————————————————————————→

1	2	3	4	5	6	7
I wish that my child were more emotionally dependent on me.			I'm happy with how emotionally dependent my child is.			I wish that my child were less emotionally dependent.

10. ←———————————————————————————→

1	2	3	4	5	6	7
I urged my child to pursue certain majors and avoid others.			I had advice about academic majors but left the decision up to my child.			I didn't care about my child's major.

11. ←———————————————————————————→

1	2	3	4	5	6	7
I miss my child all the time upon leaving home.			I miss my child sometimes.			I rarely miss my child.

12. ←———————————————————————————→

1	2	3	4	5	6	7
I expect my child to share personal issues.			I'm willing, but don't expect, to hear about my child's personal issues.			I'm not interested in hearing about my child's issues.

Answer Sheet
Test Answers

1. _____   7. _____
2. _____   8. _____
3. _____   9. _____
4. _____   10. _____
5. _____   11. _____
6. _____   12. _____

Total: _____

Score from 12 to 36 = *Change Resistance*; Score from 37 to 53 = *Change Assistance*; Score from 54 to 84 = *Change Desistance*

To rate yourself in the three areas of family functioning, fill in the score for the test item indicated and then add them:

EMOTIONS

2. _____   8. _____
5. _____   11. _____

Total: _____

Score from 4 to 9 = *Emotional Resistance*; Score from 10 to 19 = *Emotional Assistance*; Score from 20 to 28 = *Emotional Desistance*

CONTACT

3. _____   9. _____
6. _____   12. _____

Total: _____

Score from 4 to 11 = *Contact Resistance*; Score from 12 to 20 = *Contact Assistance*; Score from 21 to 28 = *Contact Desistance*

DECISION-MAKING

1. _____   7. _____
4. _____   10. _____

Total: _____

Score from 4 to 11 = *Decision-Making Resistance*; Score from 12 to 21 = *Decision-Making Assistance*; Score from 22 to 28 = *Decision-Making Desistance*

CHAPTER 4

Interpreting the Test Results

If the test revealed that you have a tendency toward change resistance, don't feel at all discouraged. The fact that you care so much about your relationship with your child and bought this book means that you're a great parent. It's just a matter of readjusting to accommodate the changes that this new phase of life demands. Also, give yourself credit for having overcome the pull of denial, and answered the questions honestly.

If you have a propensity for change assistance, the remaining information in the book can help you stay on the right track, and also offer you new alternative strategies.

If you lean more toward the change desistance end of the scale, you may be feeling that the only way to end family conflict and turmoil is for your child to go away to college. You are extra fearful, though, that relations could really drift or rip apart. It's painful for you to make yourself vulnerable to a sense of hope that the relationship can improve. It takes courage to try to make things better, and you've chosen an excellent time in your child's life to do so; the window of opportunity is here.

Within each subcategory—emotions, contact, and decision-making—there is a continuum from having major struggles to being a little bit stuck. The descriptions of parenting styles in this chapter fall more on the extreme ends of the scale, even though most of you will fall more in the middle.

The Three Main Parent Groups

Change Assisting

When you're assisting change, your child directs the show, while you provide the technical support—taking cues from your child. As a college student, your child experiences a series of challenges, from roommate troubles to rush week to final exams, with occasional calmness in between. You accommodate his extremely busy life by providing love and advice according to his needs. Sure, you're sad that he's gone, but you're also happy to have more time for yourself. When you have hardships of your own, you rely on spouses and friends to help you through. The confidence that you express in your child's ability to handle college life goes a long way; your child finds himself flourishing and feeling even closer to you than before he left home.

Change Resisting

You very much want to support your child's move to college, but your sadness over the departure can interfere at times. Although you know that the relationship with your child has to readjust to allow for her increased independence, it's hard for you to truly accept this fact. You miss your child terribly, and want to talk to her as much as possible to hear her voice and be filled in on the details of college life. Fraught with worry over your kid's safety and professional future, you may try to be an influential figure in her life, especially when it comes to important decisions, such as the academic major. When you feel overwhelmed by life's stresses, you often turn to your college-aged child for support with the hope that you can be best friends.

Underlying your attempts to maintain the status quo is the fear that college will cause family relationships to deteriorate. Unfortunately, it seems that the more you try to maintain the old closeness, the less chance the new and improved closeness has to enter the relationship. The danger here is that family relationships can start sliding downhill and your child may be too distracted to concentrate on homework. You love and care about your child; you just need to loosen your grip.

Change Desisting

If you exhibit a tendency toward change desistance, then you're probably upset about the current state of the relationship with your child. When there is a tremendous amount of conflict during the high school years, your child's departure for college can seem like a welcome relief. The good news is that the physical separation can ease tensions. The bad news is that there's a danger of using the newfound space to drift apart. You and your child will probably call and see each other infrequently and leave each other out of important life developments. With little contact, there's less and less tying you together.

The day-to-day conflict is gone, but the tension remains. You may think that your child is simply happy to be away from home and doesn't care about you, but that isn't true. Just as you care deeply about your child, and she doesn't think that you do, the reverse holds as well. Both of you feel that it's too painful to express any warmth and hope, so you keep those feelings underground. You feel at your wit's end about how to turn things around; reading this book may constitute a last-ditch effort. Chapter 8 Change Desisters: How to Keep the Family Together is dedicated solely to the issues you face. The chapter will provide concrete steps to take to turn your relationship around. This is the perfect time for renewed efforts and optimism.

The reason the majority of this book focuses on change assistance and resistance is that change desister college families are much less common than change resisters or assisters. This means that only a small number of families experience so much conflict that they can't wait for college to put some distance between them. Another reason is that when conflict overwhelms family relationships, it's hard for kids to function to the best of their potential; this means that they might not achieve college-level studies. Furthermore, these young adults may feel the need to become completely economically independent—a way of cutting all formal ties to their families; thus, full-time employment or the military may be preferable options. Not to mention the fact that parents who are looking forward to having more distance in their relationships are less likely to buy a book that quells parents' fears about separating from their kids. Yet, your child *did* make it to college and you are reading this book. Reading all the chapters in addition to Chapter 8 will give you an excellent idea of what to strive for and what to avoid when reworking your relationship.

Change Assisting and Resisting in the Three Main Areas of Family Functioning: Emotions, Contact, and Decision-Making

Parent Emotions

Change Assisting Imagine that you're tired and harried, returning home from a long day's work to the realization that, with your son at school, you don't have to prepare dinner—a smile brightens your face. On the way to the den, you pass his old room; struck by the emptiness, you begin to cry. Such are the normal ups and downs of a parent whose child has left home for college. Sadness can sweep through suddenly in waves or simply hang around as a nagging sense of melancholy. Happiness comes from different sources: seeing your child so grown-up, having more free time, or not having to fight over the volume of the stereo. A mix of emotions is natural and a healthy balance is key. Just as it takes time for students to adjust to college, so, too, does it take awhile for your emotions to settle down.

If you are skilled at communicating your feelings, you say "I miss you" in a tone that implies both "You mean a lot to me" and "I'm happy for you." You draw comfort from the fact that your family isn't alone; millions of other American college students reside at school. You allow yourself the pride that comes with having launched your child successfully into adulthood.

Change Resisting Your sadness over your child's departure overwhelms any positive emotion you might be feeling. Everywhere you turn you run into reminders of your child being gone: the sight of a teenager in baggy jeans, the sound of a rock song, the odor of sweaty socks. Your child was at the center of your life for over seventeen years and the sense of loss runs deep. The stages of your reaction to the departure are often similar to, but less intense than, the stages of grieving somebody experiences when a loved one has died; denial of the absence comes first, followed by anger at the child for leaving, and grief for the loss.

Fears that the relationship with your young adult will become emotionally distant, or even that it might end, plague you. The fact that most young adults in the United States leave home for college is little comfort, and you deny yourself the full pride that you could feel in your child and in yourself for having helped her reach college.

No matter how hard you might try to cover up your sadness and concern, your child always senses the truth—the emotional radar is quite sharp after almost two decades of living together in the same house. Your child is pleased that you love and miss him, but it's difficult for him to settle into college life when he knows that he's causing you distress. Even just a seed of self-doubt can grow insidiously fast into rampant insecurity at a time when a young adult is trying to form new relationships with roommates, friends, lovers, and professors. If thoughts of home induce in your child more feelings of stress than comfort, then he may feel stranded in a brand-new environment without a secure base. He needs your total blessing to succeed in the world as an independent person on the road to adulthood.

The challenges for you include:

- Letting yourself experience the gladness, in addition to the sadness, that this period brings.
- Allowing yourself to celebrate what you don't miss about your child being gone.
- Feeling reassured that college can help your relationship, as opposed to hinder it.

Parent-Student Contact

Change Assisting Imagine that you're watching a television program about the Civil War and think, "Oh, my daughter would love this—I should call her at school." You pick up the phone, then hesitate, "But she's probably busy studying or doing whatever," and put down the receiver without ever dialing. You miss your child, think of her often, but refrain from interrupting her hectic life. Your kid will call home when she has a free moment or needs some advice because you've let her know that she is welcome, but not expected, to call anytime. Of course you call her at school sometimes as well.

You know that there's no one right way to stay in touch, that the key is tuning into your child's cues for contact needs and following them accordingly. You have an open-door policy; your child can come home and sleep in his room anytime, but you don't expect him home more often than the occasional major holiday. If your child calls school "home," you may feel a little twinge of jealousy, but overall you're glad he feels comfortable there. When it comes to visiting your child on campus, you call ahead of time, make the visit optional, and keep the frequency to a minimum. School visits suit your kid's needs, which usually involve shopping, or revolve around university activities, such as theatre productions or sporting events.

Change assisters don't require phone or in-person contact with their children to know that family relationships still exist. By the time your kid leaves for college, you have learned from experience that as children spend increasingly greater periods of time out of the house, from sleepovers to summer camps to late-night parties, family bonds persist. Whatever personal information your child shares, you're grateful, yet careful not to pry. While you listen and support your child, you also send the message that you hope she will develop close friendships at college.

Occasionally, parents go overboard in their efforts to give students space; they call too infrequently or don't ask enough about college life. Hurt feelings and confusion may follow, but bad feelings will clear up quickly thanks to good communication skills. Remember, change assisting is a sign of a healthy family, not a perfect one. No family is perfect.

The sensitivity you show to your child's needs pays off: Your child will be inspired to contact you regularly and keep you updated on the important ups and downs of college life. Your child may still be vulnerable to setbacks, but having you as a secure base during stressful periods will help him ride through them like a surfer on the waves.

Change Resisting Just as a single person waits anxiously by the telephone for a potential date to call, you eagerly await your child's call. You long to hear his voice because it reassures you that there is still a connection— the relationship persists. If your child didn't mind, a phone call a day would feel great; in fact, no amount of contact would be too much for you. If your child has a cell phone, it's all the more difficult to resist calling, knowing that you can reach him anywhere at anytime. If your child calls a lot when college begins and less often thereafter, you worry that the decrease in frequency is the beginning of the end of family relationships, as opposed to just the normal college adaptation process. The fact that your child leads a hectic life is little comfort for you; it's hard for you not to take his contact frequency personally.

In-person visits can be a source of conflict. If your child says he has to stay at school instead of visit because he has to study, you offer, "Come home to study—I'll take care of you." Your response is well-meaning, but your child may experience it as pressure; he wants you to understand that he needs to stay on campus to have access to libraries, study groups, and late-night-fun study breaks. When your child does visit, he probably spends time studying, talking on the phone, or seeing neighborhood friends. When this happens, you tend to feel neglected, fearing that he doesn't care about you.

You care about how your child is doing at school and hope that he'll reveal what's really going on in his life. If he doesn't, you fear the worst— that he's doing terribly and that your relationship is dissolving before your eyes. Your fear can drive you to push for information, as opposed to letting it flow naturally. When your child establishes close friendships at school, you may feel threatened that your child will no longer need you. The danger of requesting a lot of contact and personal information is that you may unwittingly create a self-fulfilling prophecy: The more you ask for intimacy, the less of himself your child will want to give. Of course you want to show interest and love; the key, again, is striking a balance.

The major challenges for you include:

- Establishing an informal contact schedule that works well for both of you.
- Feeling certain of your bond with your child without having to hear his voice.
- Appreciating what your child shares with you and not worrying about what he omits.

Student Decision-Making

Change Assisting You care about your child's studying, eating, and partying habits, but figure why waste a lot of time fretting—kids will do what they do whether you worry about them or not. In fact, you worry even less than you did during the high school years; with your child out of the house, you can't keep track of his whereabouts. The old saying "What you don't know can't hurt you" comes into play.

You live by the principle that the more parents trust their children, the more responsible the kids become, and this works. On top of managing his daily life, your child has big decisions to make about finances, academic major, and more. You may harbor an abundance of opinions about what your child should and shouldn't do, but refrain from imposing them. Instead, you adopt the role of consultant, asking pointed questions based on wisdom about the world and who your child is as an individual. Through this process, he learns how to problem-solve. If you strongly disagree with his stance, you will communicate your position with respect and accept whatever choice he makes. You let him learn from his misguided choices, as well as from his successes. Solid reasoning skills are ultimately more important for success than any one decision a student will make during his college career, and you know this. You believe that taking one particular door doesn't shut other doors forever.

Calm, yet on the ball, your child has learned from you how to go with the flow and take charge. Free to learn from his own mistakes, he takes a mature, responsible approach to life. He tends to gather information from various sources, including parents, and make educated decisions that also take gut instinct into account. There are no drawbacks to consulting you on important decisions because he knows that you won't tell him what to do. When faced with disappointment, he's able to pick himself up and try again. Armed with good problem-solving skills, parental support, and resiliency, your child has a propensity for success.

Change Resisting College is the time when your worry for your child mushrooms. You believe that your child—by no longer living in the protected environment of home—is more vulnerable to outside evils (e.g., muggers) and internal weaknesses (e.g., the tendency to procrastinate). You may hear a television news report about a bank robbery in the big city where your child attends college and panic, imagining her caught in a crossfire even though she uses a different bank altogether.

Big decisions weigh heavily on your mind because you fear that bad choices can severely limit your child's future options. For example, if your child is a psychology major, you might clip all the articles you can find on how HMOs are restricting the income and job opportunities for psychologists, and send them to him. Concerns that you yourself have been closed in by the decisions you yourself made in college may add to your urgency. Frustrated by the fact that your child's well-being seems largely out of your hands, you hope that if you express your opinions strongly enough, your child will follow them.

Do college-aged kids still need their parents? Of course they do, but you can easily doubt it. Do they take on values that are radically different from those of their parents? They might, but odds are they won't, even though you worry that they will. These are a couple of the reasons that you feel reassured when your child listens to and follows your advice. You've probably developed your own approach to problem-solving, that if you taught it to your child, it could help him in a wide variety of circumstances. What prevents you from doing this is an intense investment in the actual outcome of his decisions, and a fear that he won't need you anymore.

When you express strong opinions, your child feels less affectionate and more reluctant to consult you on important decisions. He is doubly lost; he's reluctant to trust the advice you give, and if you haven't exhibited confidence in his problem-solving ability, then he's likely to mistrust himself as well. When he does finally come to a conclusion, it likely reflects your wishes or a reaction against them. Feeling disconnected from the choices he has made can lead to a lack of the resolve he needs to succeed. He may find himself stumbling along and unable to bounce back when things go wrong.

The main tasks for you in this area are:

- Learning to enjoy the fact that, for the most part, what you don't know can't hurt you.
- Identifying your own successful problem-solving strategies and enjoying teaching them to your child.
- Managing your concern so that you are able to give your child room to learn from his own mistakes.
- Showing confidence in your child's ability to handle college, even if you don't feel it 100 percent.

To Conclude

To confront the challenges listed in this chapter, read on. Pat yourself on the back for identifying the areas in which you will be working toward assisting change. The efforts you make in your relationship with your college-aged child will pay off tremendously. The gains you make will spill over into the other significant relationships in your life, because you will feel self-confident and happy, empowered to make a difference.

To Students

You've taken the Change Resistance Test and identified where each of your parents may be having trouble assisting change. Even if only one of your parents is resisting change, chaos can follow. In one family, the father refused to have his son move out of the house, while the mother aided the son's departure. The result? When the son did move out, the father blamed his wife for the departure and in response, she threatened to move out herself. I tell you this story to let you know that you're not imagining how difficult it can be, even when only one parent is resisting the transition.

Each of the remaining chapters concludes with advice addressed specifically to you. In addition, you will find solace and helpful hints in the guidance given to parents.

PART III

Assisting Change in the Three Areas of Family Functioning

Emotions, Contact, and Decision-Making

CHAPTER 5

Parent Emotions
How to Overcome Sadness

Mixed Emotions

Having a child leave for college sparks the whole range of big emotions:

- The **sadness** of missing your child, as well as the **gladness** of having more privacy and fewer home-policing duties.
- The **melancholy** of marking the end of your kid's childhood, along with the **excitement** of seeing your child embark on the journey to adulthood.
- The **regret** of wishing you had parented differently, and the **pride** of knowing that you helped your child reach this milestone.
- The **anxiety** of wondering how well your child will adjust to school, along with the **comfort** of knowing that your child is on his way to becoming self-sufficient.
- The **envy** of all the opportunities that lie ahead of your child, accompanied by the **relief** that you've already struggled through the major questions of self-identity.

For every emotion you feel, there's likely to be the opposite one lurking nearby. Mood swings are the norm. Having your kid leave for college is an emotional roller-coaster of a time. So if you feel off-kilter or like you're going crazy—wondering if early menopause has hit or whether or not men go through menopause—rest assured that what you're experiencing is normal.

This chapter will help you cope with your sadness and regret, as well as assist you in bringing more celebration and pride into the transition experience. The next chapter will tackle the worries you have for your child, and give you advice on how to best guide his college adaptation.

The Stages of Emotional Adjustment

While you're likely to experience a wide range of emotions in response to your child leaving for college, there's also a core set of feelings that will underlie your experience. The first sustained stage includes **denial:**

Harold, a dad: Sometimes I suddenly think, "Oh, where is my son?" Sometimes I go to his bedroom, and then ask myself, "But where is he right now?" I recall a lot of feeling from before. But I have to accept the fact of what it is.

You walk in the front door and think you hear your son's favorite album playing on the stereo; meanwhile, it's just the sound of your younger daughter watching TV. You put four place settings on the dinner table, but with your son out of the house, there are only three family members eating. You think you see your son in his room, but it's only his sports poster on the wall.

Have similar lapses happened to you? If so, don't worry—you're not becoming psychotic. It's just your mind playing tricks on you. Sure, part of the denial experience is due to habit: the expectations that you built up over the years. Don't fool yourself into believing that this is the whole story; you wish so much to have your child back home that your mind accommodates by making you think he's still there. Just like when thirsty people see the mirage of a watering hole in the dry, desolate desert.

The realization that your son's stereo isn't playing, that only three people are eating dinner, or that it was a poster you saw, brings with it a sense of **sadness**—sadness that your child is gone. As denial wears off and the recognition of the departure sinks in, sadness can intensify.

Change Assister Stages

If you're a change assister parent, then you let yourself experience the poignancy of these feelings. Change assister parents not only actively implement coping strategies, but also calmly let time work its healing magic. They are able to work through their sadness and enter the **acceptance** phase within a relatively brief period:

Felicia, a mom: Every time I think of him I miss him, but there is no way I would want him sitting here, because it wouldn't be good for him. I thought more about his being gone when he first left than I do now. It took me at least a couple of months to get used to it. Now, I almost take it for granted that he's not here. I'm sorry he's not here, I wouldn't mind if he were, but I try not to let my feelings interfere with his independence.

A small number of change assister parents bypass the sadness phase altogether and head right into the acceptance stage:

Rosemary, a mother: I keep waiting to miss him, but I never do. I love it when he comes home; I really enjoy having him here. He brings a lot of life to the family and everybody is happy when he's home. But when he goes back, that's fine. I really don't miss him. I'm not glad when he goes. It's not a relief to see him walk out the door, no, no, no, not at all. It's just that I don't miss him, but I really like it when he comes home.

A parent's life may be so full that she doesn't experience a significant gap with her child out of the house. She can carry around an image of her child that maintains the strong feeling of connection. Then, when her son is at home, she can be in the moment and enjoy his presence. A change assister father asked, "Does missing equal love?" and then answered his own question: "For me, I don't think so. You can always care for somebody, but you don't have to miss somebody that much." However, if you're experiencing an absence of missing accompanied by not being happy to see your child, then your relationship may be so steeped in conflict that you fall into the change desister category.

Change Resisters' Stages

If you're a parent with change resister tendencies, then you may feel over-whelmingly sad, as if someone you love dearly has died. Recall the experience of Marshall Warren who likened his son's departure to a college twenty minutes away to suffering a death in the family. Veronica equates her daughter's leaving home for college with another traumatic life transition:

It was the right thing for my child, but it was sad for us parents. It's similar to when two people who love each other get a divorce, yet neither of them really want it. It's a contradiction in terms. I think it's a huge trauma. It's huger than anyone can ever imagine.

You find yourself stuck in the muck of the sadness phase, unable to push through to acceptance. You have trouble focusing on work. You cry much more easily than usual when watching a movie or reading the paper. A mere mention of children can create a lump in your throat. You know that it would be good for you to get out of the house, do activities, see people, but you just don't feel like it. Something is missing, and nothing fills you up.

In your mind, your child's departure threatens the very existence of your parent-child bond, not to mention all the other fears you have about growing older. Separation **anxiety** can feed the sadness and vice versa.

When sadness becomes overpowering, it's **anger** to the rescue:

Jasmine, a student: When my parents dropped me off at college for the first time, I saw my father cry. I felt bad. I was like, "Dad, do you want to stay for dinner?" I felt so bad. Later, I heard from my sister that he told her, "I'm not gonna have any more daughters; they just cause me pain."

Do you find yourself resenting your child for moving out, even though deep down inside you know that he's supposed to leave? You might even entertain the notion that a large part of his plan for attending college was to be able to leave home—to leave you behind? If so, then anger is serving as a temporary defense against sadness. Anger may make you feel as if there's something that could be done to remedy the situation, "Why did she have to leave?" Sadness leaves you feeling depressed and helpless, "She's gone. There's nothing I can do."

There are two major drawbacks to letting resentment take over. It takes a toll on you because it prevents you from working through your sadness and puts physical stress on your heart. Your resentment also strains your relationship with your child, who feels caught in a double bind; she needs to grow up, but by growing up, she's hurting you. She feels like she can't win, and your relationship can easily become a source of stress and guilt for her.

Never fear, if anger and resentment have already worked their way in or sadness has taken over, this chapter will guide your emotions in a healthy direction; you will be able to push forward into acceptance.

Countering Sadness with Gladness

Change assisters' most popular coping strategy is to balance out the losses experienced with the gains. Recall the Evans parents who felt ambivalent, both "sad and glad," when their twin daughters left for college. Change assisters speak of a whole variety of gains:

Sally, a mom: *Sure I was pleased. There's less laundry, less noise, and fewer phone calls. Heather doesn't sit still, so it's a calmer household without Heather here. Heather creates a lot of confusion, so a lot of confusion is gone. Heather shared a car with her brother, so now I don't have to arbitrate who gets the car.*

Less confusion in the home, less strife between siblings, and less housework to do are just a few of the potential home improvements. There's also the simple pleasure of being able to keep track of your car keys, the TV remote control, and the sections of the newspaper you love to read. You can have access to the telephone or car when you need them and to your favorite TV shows after a long day of work. There's less staying up late at night worrying about at what ungodly hour your child will walk in the door, and less policing of homework and chore duty. If all your kids are out of the nest, then there's the joy of being able to ramble about the house naked—very liberating. If none of this sounds at all appealing to you, then you are truly steeped in change resistance, especially since family tension often builds leading up to the departure:

Richard, a dad: During the summer before college starts, parents and kids often fight, getting into hard-core clashes and stress. This is a way of distancing so that the painful separation can take place more easily.

Change resisters focus only on what they miss about their child being gone, while change assisters assess *both* their losses and their gains.

As a change resister parent, you experience the same gains as assisters, but don't allow yourself to acknowledge and enjoy them. To apply a cliché, change assisters see the glass as *both* half empty and half full, while as a change resister, you mainly see the glass as only half empty. Here's a quick "What's in the Glass?" test:

1. You have one less child at the dinner table, so you think:
   a. One less mouth to feed.
   b. One less person to help with the dishes.
   c. There will be a gap in the dinner conversation.
   d. Dinner will be calmer.
   e. All of the above.

2. You notice that the house is quieter with your child off to college, and think to yourself:
   a. At last I can hear myself think.
   b. I miss the sound of his voice.
   c. I don't miss that stereo blasting.
   d. I need some distraction.
   e. All of the above.

3. You have more free time with fewer kids to take care of on a daily basis and think:
   a. Yeah! I can pay more attention to what I need.
   b. I'm going to be bored without enough to do.

c. I'll have more time to devote to work and romance.

d. I wish I were needed more.

e. All of the above.

How did you do? Change assisters are likely to check off "All of the above," while as a resister you would tend to check off only the negative aspects of change. What keeps you from seeing the glass as half full? You may fear that a celebration of gains will signify that you love your child less or make your child's departure all too final—sealing the loss. Deep inside you see the irrationality behind these thoughts, but they keep creeping back in. You may also find that accepting the fact that you have fewer kids to care for might make you feel less needed—as if you've been downsized overnight:

Susan, a mother: *You feel bad when you say goodbye to your child when she goes off to college because you know that she is now learning to stand on her own two feet; that she doesn't need you as much as she needed you before. You feel proud of her on the one hand, but a little sad to see it happen.*

Your child still needs you to provide parental love, support, and advice. This is an important role that nobody else can replace. The university can feed your child, but can't be a nurturing parent. You and your home can be your child's safe haven: a temporary refuge from the heavy responsibilities of adulthood.

If you're having trouble relishing the benefits, here are a few actions to take.

ACTION
Enjoying the Gains

1. Make a List of All the Potential Benefits You Might Experience.

Make sure to cover family life, housework, and your own life—everything from the general, such as more free time, to the specific, such as fewer smelly gym socks showing up in odd places. Include all the ways you see how your relationship with your child could improve. Think about your past typical day versus the present; in what ways has conflict lessened since your child left home? If you haven't yet listed *at least* five gains, then consult somebody who's heard you complain over the years.

2. Celebrate Your Gains.

If you're freed up from making dinner, go out to dinner with a friend. If you no longer hear your child's stereo blasting, then listen to music, a book on tape, National Public Radio, or the birds chirping out the window; listen to what *you* want to hear.

3. Evaluate What You Think Your Child Will and Won't Miss about Living at Home.

To counter any guilt you might feel about acknowledging your gains, think about what household conflicts your child will be happy to leave behind as well. To quell your fears about losing your child, consider what your child will miss about being home.

4. Join in Your Child's Excitement.

Buy sweatshirts, baseball caps, coffee mugs, and other paraphernalia with the university name stamped on it. Follow the college's sport teams. Embrace the institution that now constitutes your child's new second home. Take the view that rather than disbanding, your family is actually expanding to include new people and institutions.

Filling Up the Holes

Celebrating the benefits gained from your child's departure shouldn't in any way indicate that the sadness you feel is insignificant. Change assister parents often experience both intense sadness and intense joy about their child's departure. What helps stabilize change assisters through the emotional storm is their firm belief that the essence of parent-child attachment won't be disrupted:

David, a dad: *The relationship you have with your child is like a peach. The outside changes; it gets bigger, but there's a core, a seed in the center that remains the same. This basic part of the relationship is forged probably between the time of birth and the time they're twelve years old. After that time, there are things that make it look one way or another; clearly we are much less a part of our daughter's daily life than we were when she was a junior in high* *school. So that part of the relationship has changed; she doesn't rely on us like she used to, but there's still that joy when we hear her on the end of the phone—a feeling that will always be there.*

Change assisters accept their sadness and let it flow when the feelings touch them. You may recall that the Evans parents talked about how they both burst into tears when they realized that everything they were saying about their twin daughters was in the past tense. As you listen to what other parents miss most about their kids being gone, think about what triggers your sadness:

Erin, a student: *My dad was sad that I wasn't there to be with him or to tease, or for us to go shopping. When we go shopping for food, we spend hours. We read everything in the supermarket, and we laugh so hard when we find some foreign food; we just laugh hysterically at what it's made out of, like seaweed, and pig's eye—it's hilarious.*

Felicia, a mom: *We were sorry to see him go 'cause he's a lot of fun to have around home. He's always playing with his younger brother and sister. He exudes a lot of positive energy. When he's here, the house just seems very full. It's not physical space I'm concerned about; it's the mental space.*

Being able to identify the specific aspects of what you miss most with your child gone can guide your coping efforts. For example, when the Evans parents discuss their twin daughters in the past tense, they could reaffirm the relationships by making a conscious effort to add references to the present and future tenses. Erin's dad could make sure that he and his daughter go food shopping whenever they get together. Felicia could hire a young babysitter who loves to play with the children. Of course there's no substitute for your child, but why shouldn't parents do what makes them feel better?

As a change resister parent, feelings of sadness are so powerful that they consume all the details of daily missing and become an amorphous blob that is hard to tackle. This next exercise will help you pinpoint what you miss most about not having your child around, and gives you suggestions for filling in the holes.

ACTION
Filling In the Holes

1. Take Comfort in Your Sadness.

Your missing your child is a testament to the positive attachment you feel toward her.

2. Acknowledge What You Miss.

To aid the analysis: Take a walk through your home and pause in each room, imagining what life was like in that room before and after your child's departure. Look through photo albums. With your spouse, discuss the nature of your lives before and after your child's departure.

3. Let the Tears Flow.

At any moment when you feel so sad that tears well up in your eyes, let them flow. Crying is a physical and emotional release; you just might smile afterwards. At the very least, you can laugh at all the tissues you used up.

4. Make a List of What You Miss about Your Child and How to Fill In the Holes.

   a. If you love spending a particular type of time with your child, then schedule that into whatever visits you may have, whether it's playing tennis or going shopping. Be creative; if you were movie buddies, then send her movie reviews, watch the films separately, and talk about them over the phone.

   b. If you miss having warm bodies in the home, then find ways to open your doors to people by starting a book club, or inviting people over for a dinner party or a night of card games. Buy a cordless headset telephone and talk to friends and relatives while you're doing chores around the house.

   c. If your house feels too big now, too many empty rooms, then turn a spare room—*not* the one just vacated by your child—into an office or crafts room. If you really want to be a big hit with your kid, create a game room with a pool or ping-pong table, a stereo, and well-stocked mini fridge; your home could easily become the hub for your child and her friends when she visits.

5. Be Especially Good to Yourself.

This is a rough transition time, so give yourself a break. If you make more mistakes at work than usual or you're moody at home, chalk it up to your child's departure. Then take long, luxurious baths, go for strolls in the evenings, or rent a good movie.

6. Put Up Photos of Your Child.

It's nice to be reminded of your connection with your child.

Gathering Support

Another popular coping mechanism for change assister parents is obtaining emotional support from other adults. Because these parents aren't self-conscious about the fact that they're having trouble with their children's home-leaving, they're able to reach out to others who are in a similar situation. Sharing the struggles and triumphs of this period with a spouse and friends has a calming effect:

Kathleen, a mom: We had our friends who were in the same position of having their kids leave for college, and I think that was a big help. Just hanging out and commiserating with our other friends, checking out that they feel the same way we do, and you know you're not acting significantly different than some of the other parents.

Having little social support exacerbates feelings of change resistance.

While change assister parents garner support, as a change resister parent you often feel alone in your despair. You enter the transition already feeling isolated, and your sadness makes you feel even more so. Perhaps your sadness feels so overwhelming that you can't imagine sharing it with somebody else because you picture washing the person away in your flood of tears. Or maybe you've unconsciously transformed your sadness into resentment toward the very person or people who could provide comfort.

What may also be contributing to your sense of isolation is that all the other parents you know seem to be coping just fine. Even if other parents appear calm, cool, and collected on the outside, this doesn't mean that they really are on the inside. Everybody has a private self that differs from what they show publicly. The majority of the parents whose kids are leaving for college feel saddened, even if their child's school is nearby. Knowing that you are not alone should help you take the following steps to reach out for support.

ACTION
Sharing Your Trials and Tribulations

1. **Turning to Your Significant Other.**
   a. If you have a romantic partner in your life, share with each other your reactions to the departure. Perhaps he can help you get more in touch with your gladness and, in turn, you can help him get in touch with his sadness.
   b. Recommend that your spouse read this book as a basis for your discussion. If a direct request fails, then read the book in bed next to him and give a lot of audible, hmms, ahhhs, and light chuckles. Or place a bookmarker in a passage you think he would find particularly interesting, then casually leave the book in various places around the house. If he bites the bait, then buy him his own copy so that he can take the test in private. Suggest that you try a few of the exercises together.
2. **Gather Parents in Similar Situations.**
   a. Parents going through the same transition are probably as eager as you are to share their experiences. If you're already close to other parents of beginning college students, then gather them. If not, then reach out to parents of your child's friends; this option is especially fun and comforting because when you reminisce, each parent will recall stories about each other's kids.
   b. When you contact the parents, suggest that you meet every other week on a regular basis until you're all over the emotional hump. Even just meeting with one person can help. To get the group discussion started, you could recommend that they read this book.
   c. Other alternatives include checking with your local church or synagogue to see if they host an "empty nest" group, or chatting with other parents of college students on the Internet. If you don't already have Internet access in your home, you can go to a public library or treat yourself to a home set-up.
3. **Seek Out Professional Guidance.**
   If this life phase is bringing up a lot of intense feelings about your family

relationships and the rest of your life, seeking professional help might be a better way to go. Many people use counseling as a way to help them through difficult transition times. I call this "tune-up time"—just as you bring your car in for regular checkups, sometimes you need an emotional readjustment.

Managing Extenuating Circumstances

The Issues That Arise

While change assister parents generally have an easier time gathering a support team around them, change resisters are more likely to be struggling with extenuating circumstances that lessen their support just at the time they need it most. It's not uncommon for parents of college-aged kids to be coping with the physical decline and even death of their own parents. If the loss is fresh, the stages of mourning you experience—denial, anger, sadness, and acceptance—will overlap with the emotions you go through related to your child's departure.

For immigrant parents who have left most of their family behind overseas, having their children leave home can be particularly poignant—a feeling that the family diaspora will never stop. Or if the parents have difficulty speaking English, they may have come to depend on their children for language assistance.

Professional Stress

With more and more families experiencing mobility due to job opportunities, it wouldn't be unusual if you were adjusting to geographical changes and family physical separation. If the effort you put into parenting helped make up for your unhappiness at work, then having your child leave will be difficult. It's also possible that you came to rely on your child as your main comforter in regard to work stress:

Adam, a student: My mom, she'll get upset about the different problems at work. She'll call me just to tell me about it. I'll give her advice—what I think she should do. Sometimes it gets to the point where she doesn't want to go to work. And I just tell her you should talk to your boss and get it straight.

Considering that it's much healthier for a peer to support you than a child, your kid's departure is a good opportunity for you to find support elsewhere. Facing your career unhappiness will be difficult, but making professional changes will brighten your path.

Stay-at-Home Parents

How does your balance of work versus childcare play into how it is for you when your child leaves home? As you probably guessed, the more time of your day that you spent organizing your life around child-rearing—not just childcare, but also parent-teacher meetings, school fundraisers, driving your child to soccer practice, etc.—the more jarring his departure will be for you. The greater the impact of the home leaving, the greater the odds that you will experience change resistance.

The key to being a stay-at-home change assister parent is to face head-on the fact that there is going to be a tremendous upheaval in your life—to brace yourself for it and prepare. Embark on a professional adventure: Start on a brand-new career path, go back to school for an undergraduate or a more advanced degree, build up your volunteer career, or try to pick up where you left off in your previous endeavors.

You can feel daunted by all you no longer know. You had worked your way up to being an expert parent. Unless you start your own website "ParentingAdvice.com," or work directly with kids, you'll find that you will probably need to learn a new set of skills. On the positive side, you have a good deal of life experience behind you and if you're thirsty to learn, your pace can be quick.

Pamper yourself the way you did your kids. You spent all that time helping your child manage her life; wouldn't you just love for someone to assist you at this junction? You could hire a personal fitness trainer, a house cleaner, a masseuse, a dietitian to advise on nutrition, even a decorator to redo the house.

Dads

While it's mostly mothers who are homemakers or who arrange their work schedules to be there when their children come home from school, dads often face a different dilemma. Because most dads work long hours, they weren't able to be there when their kids got home from school full of stories of their day. Also, men are trained in our society to be active problem-solvers more than sounding boards. When kids are younger they tend to prefer having a parent to be a sounding board, but as they grow older, they appreciate more and more the practical advice dads can offer. Then college comes along, bringing with it issues of finance and career—long the province of dads. This means that a father loses his child from the home just at the point when he's feeling most cherished.

In the film Indiana Jones: The Last Crusade, Indiana Jones discusses his childhood with his dad, Dr. Jones, while they're having a drink in a passenger blimp, trying to escape danger:

Indiana Jones: *Do you remember the last time we had a quiet drink? I had a milk shake.*
Dr. Jones: *What did we talk about?*
Indiana Jones: *We didn't talk. We never talked.*
. . .
Dr. Jones: *You left just when you were becoming interesting.*

Birth Order
While reading this book you may be wondering, "Who struggles more, a parent whose first or last child is leaving?" Good question. If you're prone to feeling particularly anxious when facing new circumstances, then having your first child leave may prove to be the hardest for you. If sadness and longing are your vulnerabilities, then having your last child leave may be the biggest challenge. Coping with the departure of an only child may give you a double whammy of intense anxiety and sadness. Keep in mind, though, that these are not hard and fast rules; each child plays a unique role in your life, making it more or less difficult for you to have him leave.

Marital Stress
Many American parents who are single or divorced are confronting their child's departure without the support of a spouse. If you're currently experiencing a separation or divorce, then be aware that the average emotional adjustment period is two years. A divorce *and* a child leaving home will combine to present quite a challenge. You can handle it, but give yourself leeway to have many ups and downs.

Maybe your marriage is in limbo and you fear that with your child leaving, the partnership will take a turn for the worse:

Jasmine, a student: When I was leaving for school, I could tell that she wasn't comfortable with the idea of me leaving because of her relationship with my dad. Sometimes my mom would say, "Your dad and I are staying together just because of the kids." This was one of the things that made the year more difficult—I was pretty torn apart by that.

Perhaps your child plays a role in mediating your marital troubles:

Andrea, a student: My parents have always fought a lot. I'm just surprised that they're still married. My mom and I, we're really close emotionally and she'll always tell me when she has a big problem with my dad. I try to be there for her but it's kind of weird to have your mother leaning on you like that. But I try to do what I can for her to help her out.

Living in an unhappy marriage can be tormenting, and turning to a child for comfort and affirmation can feel like well-deserved, innocent moments of solace. The problem is that this takes a heavy toll on your child; one sophomore in the study who buckled under the strain of being in the middle of her parents' unhappy marriage flunked out of college.

By advising a parent on marital problems, or simply just listening to the parent's complaints, the child feels as if she is betraying the other parent. Even if you feel that your spouse is in the wrong, it's best for your child that she feel like she has two protectors in the world. Remember, your spouse may be a lousy partner, but it doesn't mean that he doesn't have something positive to offer as a parent. Having warm relationships with all parents increases the odds that your child will have a happy life.

Students serve merely as Band-Aids; their well-intended assistance provides superficial comfort, while at the same time warding off the possibility of the genuine healing of a professional. Existing in an unhappy marriage prevents you from moving on and finding happiness either on your own or with a different partner. If it's your kids that you're worried about, kids thrive better if parents are happy, yet apart, rather than unhappy and together. It's easier for you to be a good parent when you're feeling content in your own life. Use this junction in life to increase your odds for achieving romantic satisfaction, whether it be by going with your partner for a dose of couple's therapy or experimenting with a trial separation.

Shielding Your Child from Marital Discord

It makes sense that on average, change assisters' marriages tend to be happier than those of change resisters. Unhappily married parents are more scared of what future changes will bring, so they cling to the status quo, the working assumption being that the bad that you know seems less noxious than the bad you don't know.

Happily married change assister parents work together well in the parenting department and convey a sense of partnership to their kids:

Lynne, a mother: *My husband and I said we would be friends first and parents after that. We know parents who had five kids, and when the last one left home they fought like cat and dog; they just didn't know each other because their life had been their kids. We decided we're not gonna be like that; we're gonna be a couple. Children are very important for the marriage, but the essentials are husband and wife because we will be helping each other for the rest of our lives.*

There are, however, change assister families with dissatisfied unions at their core. The key is that these parents make sure to keep their marital troubles separate from their relationships with their children:

Andrew, a father: *Jimmy is not too tuned in to what's going on, and if he were, he would be more a victim of the problems rather than a solution. He wouldn't want to be a referee to any of the problems that Stacey and I were having; he would carefully extract himself from that role and that's appropriate. Or I will tell him not to butt his nose in.*

The following action will help you address your fears about what will happen to your own life with your child gone, as well as cope with any extenuating circumstances.

ACTION
Coping with Extenuating Circumstances

1. Tackle Your Feelings Head-On.

Do you still have unresolved feelings surrounding a loved one's death or a divorce? If so, now would be the time to try to resolve them because they can interfere with your accepting your child's new phase of life. Self-help books, websites, and seeing a counselor can help you work through residual conflict.

2. Get Your Professional Life Back on Track.

a. Make a pros and cons list about your job and think about what you can do to diminish the cons. Consider asking for a change of responsibilities and/or for a sponsored educational class to add to your credentials and skills. If you feel locked into your job in order to put your child through college, then start planning on the side for what you will do when she graduates or you retire.

b. Consider a career switch. Learning new skills all throughout your life helps keep you feeling young; "Wow! I did that! I must be agile and vigorous." Where to begin? Dig into your old bag of dreams. If those have since evaporated, then look into career counseling through books, websites, and in-person centers for people of all ages. Feeling a glass ceiling due to age? Have an "I can do attitude." Start your own business; with the explosion of the Internet, anything is possible. Go back to college or graduate school. Wouldn't it be fun to discuss study tips with your child? I don't, however, recommend taking classes at his university; that sounds like a set-up for a TV sitcom.

c. Communicate to your child what you like about your job, as well as the drawbacks. This way she can feel excited about her future in the workforce, and not feel guilty about pursuing professional happiness when you're so unhappy.

3. Steer Your Marriage in the Right Direction.

a. With your spouse, share your hopes and fears for how you two will get along with your child gone. Discuss what your relationship was like before having kids versus after. Make sure to include what you miss about the old days and ideas for recapturing those old sparks. Remind yourselves of all those dreams you had together before the kids—living in Paris for six months, starting a business together, buying a cabin in the woods—and make them come true.

b. Create new couple rituals. All the rituals that brought you together on a regular basis probably revolved around the kids. Decide on daily and weekly events that you will share, whether it be eating breakfast and dinner together, taking a walk or jog, having a regular Saturday night date, a bath together before bed, or a special hobby you can share. Find a new vacation spot that is just for the two of you.

c. Spice up your sex life. Talk about what attracted you to the other when you first got together. Look at old photos of you as a couple. Recall the sexiest times you had together. Describe your sexual fantasies. Take a trip to lingerie or sex-toy shops. Read out loud from a book of erotic writings. Rent steamy films with great sex scenes and recreate them.

d. It can be liberating to ask yourself, "Do I want to stay married?" Answering "Yes" is a reaffirmation of your commitment to working through the problems. If you answer "No" or "Don't know," then it can't hurt to visit a couple's therapist together. Think of all the years you've invested in the marriage; what's a little more time to make sure that ending it is really what you want? Handling the fear of possibly splitting after all these years can be overwhelming; consider seeking individual therapy for yourself to get you over the hump. If your marriage ends, then this affords you more chances for happiness in the long run, even if in the short term, it's very painful.

e. Reassure your child by acting as a unit. Whether or not your marriage is strong or dissolving, you can still relieve your child of worry and feelings of responsibility by coming across as a team. Work out marital differences behind the scenes.

4. Give Yourself a Hug.

However corny this may sound, you're going through an especially rough time and need some tender loving care.

Taking Comfort in the Life Cycle Perspective

When change assister parents talk about their sadness over their child's departure, they always add a tag line—"Leaving home was inevitable." They say this with calm acceptance in their voice. They understand that being a parent means undergoing a series of stages in which you and your child renegotiate the balance between connection and autonomy. A parent's job is never done; the job description just keeps changing:

Sally, a mother: I was a little sad when she left, because it was gonna be quieter here without her. But I was pleased, because I knew how much fun she was gonna have. It was just another new challenge that she was ready for and excited about. Everything has always evolved around "the next step." After the primary grades, you go on to the intermediate grades, then into high school. College is "the next step" in her maturity, and in her life. I shed tears when she went off on her first day of kindergarten, and I shed tears when she went off to college.

Change assister parents see having their kids leaving home for college as the height of parental achievement according to American standards. In line with Charles Darwin's theory of evolution, the ultimate goal of parenting is to raise kids who will not just survive, but also thrive—college is a critical step in this process.

American collegiate life is almost synonymous with leaving home, and change assisters accept this as the bottom line. The difference between high school and college that stands out the starkest is the image of living at home versus in the dorms. Sure, if you look at the academics there are contrasts, but it's the independent living—being responsible for their own self-care and studying—that stands out the most.

In many other countries, such as India and China, young adults are likely to live at home when attending college and not move out until at least marriage, or maybe never. In Britain, there's a greater possibility than in the United States that kids will leave home even younger than college—for boarding school. So, if you're a change resister wishing you had moved to China right before the college transition, be glad that at least your child didn't attend boarding school.

Intellectually you know that leaving home for college is the norm, but emotionally you fight against it. You can't quite visualize the new parental job description, so you think that the next step is akin to falling off a cliff. Do you ever entertain the thought, "Why can't my child live at home and attend college, just as she did in high school?" Maybe you fantasize about building a little addition onto your home to accommodate your child's increasing need for privacy. You envision him having his own car and with it the freedom to come and go as he pleases. You figure that with free room and board, a well-stocked fridge, home-cooked meals, quiet study time, and parental loving care when he's under the weather, what's not to love?

Your luxurious home life would be even better than a deluxe dorm, would it not? Not. Where are the pizza pig-out parties, all-night study groups, "X-File" popcorn fests? How is she going to be up-to-date on the latest political goings-on on campus or receive that note from a secret admirer? Without all the fun and camaraderie, how is she going to get through those many rigorous hours of studying and the stress that comes from knowing that her performance is being compared to hundreds of others? Change assister parents may wish that their kids could stay home, but they don't even entertain the fantasy since they know living at school is the only way for their child to get the full college experience.

Change assister parents assume that while their kids will have a whole range of emotional reactions to starting college, it's the parents who will be doing more of the missing: They accept that this is the natural order of the family life cycle:

Polly, a student: *Parents are gonna miss their kids a lot more than their kids will miss them. Because the person who's gone is experiencing new things that keep her busy and occupied. When I was a junior in high school, my boyfriend had gone away for five weeks to China, so I couldn't even call or write. I was so miserable the whole time. And then he got back, and the next day, I left for a week. And when I got back, he said that he missed me more in the one week that he was at home than he did the whole five weeks in China. It was because I wasn't there to go do stuff with him.*

Of course it's always possible that the person who leaves the comforts of home entering a completely foreign environment will experience a harsh bout of homesickness, but this will subside as she becomes familiar with her new surroundings.

Even though you can grasp the notion that leaving home for college is the norm and that parents will be doing more of the missing, here are a few tips on how to make this knowledge really sink in.

ACTION
Putting Your Child's Leaving in Perspective

1. Congratulate Yourself on Your Achievement.

According to American standards of parenting, you have achieved the ultimate—launching your child into the college years. Also remind yourself that your job is far from over.

2. Experience How the College Transition Is Like One of Many You've Already Managed.

    a. Think back to when you dropped your child off for her first day of school ever. How were you feeling? How long did it take you to adjust? What helped you cope? How did your parenting job description change and how did it remain the same? Now ask yourself the same questions about what it was like the first time your child left on a long vacation or for summer camp.

    b. Ponder how you knew that these big steps toward separation that your child undertook were inevitable. Then ask yourself why leaving home for college in this country would be any different. Let yourself experience how the American culture sweeps your family up in its normative timetable.

3. Expect That Your Child Won't Be as Sad as You Are about the Parting.

Can you recall a time in your life when you went away leaving someone you loved behind? Now, can you think of an instance where you were the one being temporarily left behind? How did you feel in each situation? Now translate your experiences to your child's current situation.

4. Symbolically Mark the Life Cycle Transition.

Have a special family dinner. Give your child a photo album showing your child growing up through the years. Take a weekend family trip back to where you used to go when your child was young. Present your child with a special gift, whether it's something that marks the continuance with the past, such as a family heirloom, or an item that marks the future.

Monitoring How You Communicate Your Emotions

The most important aspect of your emotional reaction to your child's departure is how you relate your feelings. Even if you wish that your child wasn't leaving, you can manage to give her a genuine blessing in moving on:

Felicia, a mother: *I didn't let him see the sad. I just said, "That's great. You've got everything squared away. You'll do well." I don't want him to see that other part 'cause then he might be a little uneasy there, thinking, "How's Mom?" or that kind of thing.*
Roy, the son: *My mom was very good about not showing me how she felt about it. My brother and my dad told me as soon as she left the dorm she was crying. She was really upset.*

Not every parent would win an Oscar for the supporting role as holding-it-together parent. Especially since your own kid can be a demanding audience; he knows you well, so he's not easily fooled. As a parent, you shouldn't cover up all your sadness anyway, just enough so that your child knows that you're not going to have an emotional collapse. In fact, kids like some indication that they're going to be missed, at least a little:

Pamela, a student: *I'm happy that they're happy and I'm sad that they're sad. I'm also happy that they're sad because it means they miss me. If my mom missed me too much, that would make me feel really that I was doing something wrong; I was hurting my mom. And if she didn't miss me enough, I would feel like I was abandoned. So I'm glad that it feels just right.*

It's all a matter of balance. Kids want to know you care, but they don't want to think they've left a gaping hole in your life. Too much emotion on your part may feel like a secure base reversal to your child. Too little emotion expressed may make your child feel like she has no secure base at all. Once again the burden falls on you, the parent; you have the challenging job of managing your emotions to foster her positive feelings, while she's free to emote in response to starting college. This is what happens when you sign on to parenthood; it's a long haul of responsibility and makes demands on your maturity, but it's also potentially your most satisfying accomplishment.

College students like to know that their parents miss them, but not an overwhelming amount.

When parents' emotional communication is tipped way over toward the distraught side, their kids are unhappy:

Denise, a student: My mom cries a lot when she calls up and leaves messages on my machine. She's like somebody who's lost her puppy dog. She's always saying, "You left me here with the boys (my dad and brother); I have no one to talk to." She is really unhappy and it makes me feel guilty and selfish; she just doesn't understand. This makes me sad, because I'm happy to be out on my own.

The danger is that if your child feels like she's breaking your heart, her adjustment and your relationship will suffer. Guilt is a powerful, destructive force. Consciously she will want to flourish at school, but unconsciously she will think, "How can I settle into school when it's hurting Mom and Dad so much?"

Moms Versus Dads

Women are raised to express their emotions in our society. Dads often miss their kids as much as moms do, but typically don't express it as much. Students often find themselves scrutinizing their fathers' facial expressions and vocal tones for signs of being missed:

Larry, a student: He doesn't show his emotions as much as my mom. He would be strong, but I can kind of tell that he misses me. Every time I come home he has this big smile on his face. He keeps to himself, so a big smile means a lot. Sometimes when I call home he'll be like, "Hi Larry!" He'll really brighten up. He's really excited to hear my voice.

Of course for every rule there are exceptions. There are fathers who tell their children directly, "I miss you," and mothers who are difficult to read. Nevertheless, the opposite is definitely more the norm. Whether you're a mother or a father, the following action will help you manage your feelings so that you can relate to your child in a way that communicates, "I love you. I miss you. And I'm fine."

ACTION
The Emotional Balancing Act

1. Put Yourself in Your Child's Shoes.

Picture yourself moving out of your parents' house; how did they react? Is this something you would like to repeat or avoid with your child? Use your empathy to strike the proper balance. Remind yourself that letting your sadness flow unchecked will only push your child away.

2. Share Warm Feelings.

Take your kid by surprise; when she least expects it, say, "I love you," "I'm proud of you," "College is so exciting," and "I'm going to miss you." Just because it's not cool for your kid to become all warm and gushy in response doesn't mean that she doesn't feel it. Kids have their own "I'm calm, cool, and collected" role to act, and quite frankly, they're often better thespians than their parents.

3. Use Humor to Diffuse Awkward Moments.

For example, if your child suspects that you're doing a cover-up job on your emotions, say, "You're pretty wise. I need acting lessons, don't I?" In addition, tell him that you'll be fine; it will just take a little time to adjust.

4. If You're Generally Very Emotional, Don't Stray Too Far from Your Usual.

If you cry easily often, then you wouldn't want your child to think that a TV movie mattered more than he does.

5. If You Know Certain Partings Will Be Difficult for You, Then Warn Your Child Ahead of Time.

Rather than stress over the possibility that you might lose it in front of your child, prepare your child; say, "I'll be shedding tears of sadness and gladness. I'll do my best not to embarrass you. Don't think for a second that I don't support you in this move; I think it's the most wonderful thing and wouldn't want it any other way."

Coming to Terms with Regret

Regret may also be preventing you from emotionally moving onto the next family life cycle stage; do you wish you had a chance to do a better parenting job? Do you get hung up on the "If onlys"? If only I had come home earlier from work. If only I had played ball with him more. If only I had spent more time reviewing his homework with him. If only . . . if only . . .

Every parent has at least a few misgivings. Here's a change assister's perspective:

Greg, a dad: *The important question isn't "What kind of job did I do?" It's "Is he now prepared to face the world?" A couple of years ago I didn't know for sure. Today I could say, he certainly is. So, I am much more quieted about that.*

Here's a resister family's, the Warrens', view:

Elizabeth, the mother: *I feel a little guilty about Sam. I feel that I could have done better, or I should have done better, or I should have known more, or I should have reacted in a different way. In retrospect, I feel I could have been a better mother.*

Change assister parents expect that their parenting job isn't going to be perfect. They can let go of the past and move on. As a change resister, you look back, scared that any mistake you might have made will have permanently damaged your child and the relationship between you two. Your fears probably outweigh the actual consequences. Besides, this book is all about the new family relationship opportunities that college brings. It's easier to move optimistically toward the future when you've put past demons to rest. So why not tackle your regret head-on? Here's how.

ACTION
Saying Goodbye to Regret

1. Think Back over the Years and Note at Which Points You Wish You Had Chosen an Alternative Parenting Course.

For each regret, write down what motivated you at the time: what you learned from your own parents, an interfering crisis situation, blinded for personal reasons, inexperience, or simply poor judgment?

2. Forgive Yourself for All the Mistakes You Made.

Remind yourself that parenting is the hardest job you will ever have. Every parent makes mistakes.

3. Learn from Your Mistakes.

If there is something you wish you hadn't done, such as chastise your child for bringing home a bad grade, then try hard not to do a similar action in the future. If there's something you wish you had done, such as be more open with your love, then think about what would be an age-appropriate way of doing this now. Now is the perfect time to experiment with new ways of relating because it's less awkward to make changes when there's some physical distance between you.

4. Consider Apologizing to Your Child.

   a. It never hurts to say you're sorry and it feels very liberating. For example, maybe you secretly searched your son's room once, finding something controversial, and he's never trusted you since. You could apologize for the instance and joke that your son must be happy that you don't have the key to his dorm room; humor, especially being able to laugh at yourself, works wonders. Then promise that you will make every effort to respect his privacy in the future.

   b. Don't put the burden on your child to forgive you. Your goal is to make a generous gift of your apology and not expect anything directly in return. The rewards will come in the form of how your child feels toward you in the future; hopefully he'll be warmer and more trusting.

   c. Don't feel dismissed. It may take a lot for you to get your courage up to apologize. Even if your child says, "Oh Dad, I don't know what you're talking about," the fact that you thought it important enough to apologize will stay with him. Plus, you'll serve as an excellent role model for how one can take responsibility for one's own actions. This will encourage your child to do the same with you and others someday too.

5. Make a List of "I'm Glad I Dids."

Note what you wouldn't want to change about your parenting, even if you had the chance to do it all over again. Write down what you did as a parent that you're proud of. Maybe it was the fact that you made a special effort to be home from work in time for the family dinner, or that you put your child to bed with a kiss, or that you showed interest in her school work.

To Students

1. If Your Parents Are Grieving over Your Departure, Take Comfort. . . .

No parent has ever died from a broken heart suffered when her child left home for college. Even change resister parents overcome their grief eventually. Take comfort in the fact that you are doing what kids your age are supposed to do—go away to college. Holding yourself back would not only hurt you, but would also indisputably stunt the growth of your relationship with your parents. Are you planning to stay home forever? Your parents will have to cope with your departure at some point, so why not have it be at a time when all the other parents are coping as well.

2. If Your Parents Are Gushing with Sadness, Tell Them to Get a Grip.

a. Humor can come in handy: "Mom, any more tears and I'll need an umbrella," or "You can come to school with me, but studying for exams isn't much fun, not to mention pulling all-nighters."

b. Tell them that you know of other parents who have had similar reactions and recovered well. Subtly inform them that you've heard of this book called *Bringing Home the Laundry* that helps parents through the transition. Remember, though, it's your parents' job to cope with your departure; it shouldn't and can't be your responsibility.

3. If You Wish Your Parents Would Demonstrate More Emotion, Then . . .

a. Feel reassured by the fact that missing isn't an essential ingredient of parental love and that your parents may be putting on a good show.

b. Be a role model for emotional expression. If you miss your parents, tell them so, along with a hug and kiss hello and goodbye. They may eventually loosen up and follow suit.

c. Make sure that you're giving them the chance to miss you. Are you phoning or E-mailing them every day? Visiting every week? Cut down a bit and see what happens.

4. Homesickness Is Perfectly Normal.

Missing your family is a typical reaction to being thrown into a completely new environment. Rather than see it as a sign of weakness, view it as a sign of feeling positively connected to your family. Eventually, you will find people at school who will help make the university feel like a second home.

5. Reversing a Secure Base Reversal.

If you feel like your parents rely on you for support when they're stressed out about work or their marriage then:

a. Announce to your parents that you love them and want to strengthen your relationship with them, and that integral to this goal is that you not be their confidant and consultant on personal matters. You want general updates on their lives, but with boundaries.

b. Fight off any guilty concerns that you are abandoning or harming your parent. First of all, you're saying, "I'm still here and want to have a warm, loving relationship with you." Second of all, they will be better off in the long run without depending on you for support. Recall how Marshall Warren felt that he would never have addressed his career dissatisfaction if his son Sam hadn't left home for college.

c. Your parents will still love you. They may be angry with you for a while, not understand what on earth you're talking about, and even try to get you to fulfill the role again. Eventually, the turmoil will settle down and you can enjoy healthier parent-child relationships.

d. If you're seriously worried about your parent's well-being, then share your concerns with other people who are close to your parent. But remember you can't be the rescuer yourself and can't be in charge of gathering a reluctant rescue team. Ultimately, the only way your parent can improve her situation is if she herself is open to professional assistance. You do not have the powers to make her better or make her seek assistance, no matter how smart and insightful you are.

CHAPTER 6

Parent-Student Contact
How to Stay in Touch

Back when your child was an infant, he was unable to crawl, unable to leave your side and always wanting to be near you. With each new step of independence, from crawling, to walking, to starting school, to hanging out with friends, he spent more and more time apart from you. By the end of high school, your child might have become mostly a blur whizzing in and out of the house, going from school to home to basketball practice to home to a friend's:

David, a father: When my daughter was a little girl, she would always want to do things with us and then she got a boyfriend and she always wanted to do things with him. I told my wife, when you have kids you should spend as much time as you can with them while they are little 'cause when they grow up they have their own things to do.

Depending upon your child's lifestyle, the changes in amount of contact you're experiencing will be more or less drastic. If your child was a homebody, then the transition is going to be all the more difficult. Think back to the times in the past when your child spent more and more time away from you. How did you stay connected? Didn't you always adapt to the situation and manage to find new ways of keeping the bond intact? College is no exception, and with telephones, cell phones, beepers, E-mail, and snail mail at your disposal, in addition to cars, trains, buses, and planes, there's no reason that you and your child can't develop a contact plan that works for everybody.

Most parents are tempted to phone their kids often, especially when they first leave for school. As a parent, you want to gauge how your child is adjusting, which is difficult to keep up with when his mood is changing so frequently. You want to be there for him when he needs comfort and support, as well as ease your own worried mind. You miss your child and simply want to hear his voice. If you're a change resister, you want contact as confirmation that your relationship is still important to your child.

The key question isn't how much temptation you feel to contact your child; it's how you act on it that counts. Feelings of change resistance may be clouding your ability to separate your child's needs from your own. This chapter will help you access your instincts about what you already know is best for your child, as well as learn to read your child's cues for contact. You will be able to increase the odds that your child will be happy to hear from you and help your relationship grow.

Communicating Over a Distance: Telephone, E-Mail, and More

Determining the Appropriate Balance

The Change Assister Approach Striking a healthy balance of contact involves following both your heart *and* your head. There's no precise formula; it's a matter of finding what works best for your child. When a parent and student talk every day it is most likely an indication of parental change resistance, but could also be a result of the student having an especially difficult adjustment period. A parent and student who talk only once a month, most likely represents change desistance, but it could also be that the child is getting carried away by college. Then there are all the variations in between. Change assisters let their secure base instincts be their guide:

Felicia, a mom: I'd like Roy to call more, and I'd like to see him more, but at the same time, I'm not terribly surprised that he's not calling or visiting more because I realize that his whole life, his interests are there at school. He's not worrying about us all the time, and he shouldn't be. I'd like to hear from him every day, but I know I'm not going to. It might be bad if I heard from him every day because it might mean that he's unable to stand on his own two feet.

Even a change assister approach can be taken to a well-intentioned, but unhealthy extreme:

Sally, a mom: Last year I didn't call Heather very much because I tried to leave a little more of the calling to her so that I wouldn't be infringing on what she does. But this year, she's asked that I call more. Heather teased me and said, "You're known as the mother who doesn't care because you don't call enough." So this year I told her I would start calling more, and so I did. She said she likes messages left in the machine, so I call and leave messages.

It is not uncommon for change assister parents to make the mistake of calling too little in the beginning. They are so intent on not intruding in their child's life that they bend over backwards to avoid it. Students will feel like the rug is pulled out from under them—no secure base—and a tad abandoned. Usually this misunderstanding gets cleared up by the kid letting the parent know, "Pay more attention to me!" Then everybody laughs about how good intentions can be misguided. As I've said, change assister parents are headed in the right direction, but they aren't perfect; no parent is or can be. When you're in doubt as to whether or not a plan of action is working, simply ask your child.

The Change Resister Approach If you're resisting change, then you're often left feeling disappointed that you and your child don't talk enough. This unfulfilled desire to connect may lead you to contact your child too frequently:

Samantha, a student: She calls me almost every day, which I think is a lot. Sometimes I'll just say, "Oh hi. I have class. Yeah, I went to a party last night; it was fun. Okay, well, I'll talk to you tomorrow." So we do talk a lot,

*and sometimes I don't like saying that because I think people get the impression
that I can't be away from her.*

Granting your child some space gives your child a chance to miss you and
appreciate you, and vice versa.

Students are feeling demands being made on them from all directions.
Their professors want them to soak up the knowledge in half a textbook
for an exam in two weeks. Their roommates want them to tie up the
phone less. Their friends want them to go out and have fun more. Their
extracurricular club wants them to take on more responsibility. If on top
of all that parents want them to call more, then the parents become just
one more demand. Wouldn't you much rather be the safe haven your child
can turn to for relief from his other pressures—somebody who empathizes
with all the pressure he feels and can problem-solve with him on how to
lessen it?

Rather than take your child's not calling often personally, take what
you know about the situation and his personality into account. Has his
homesickness worn off? Is he swept away by the excitement of college?

Michael, a student: *The first few months I was here at college, I didn't
really take the time to call home, just because everything was new for me and
fun. You kind of screw around and break away from all your old ties in all
your past life—you try to establish your new identity. And then you get insecure about that and try to latch on to the things that are secure in your life. In
my case, those happen to be my parents and my girlfriend. This was my first
time living out of the house, so of course I'm going to be very excited about it,
caught up in it; I knew that I would eventually slow down and then come back.*

Does he dislike talking on the phone altogether? Perhaps he's a little
spacey, lazy, or irresponsible?

Anthony, a student: *I tend to waste a lot of time up here doing a lot of
stupid stuff, like just watching TV instead of calling my mom. She calls me at
least once or twice a week. My mom always tells me to call, she's always
saying, "You gotta call me, write me," and I never do. I'm pretty lazy. I don't*

want my mom and dad to feel this way, but my personality isn't going to change—that's just one of my inherent traits.

If this sounds like your child, it's far too late to mold him into a wonderfully responsible kid, so go with the flow; and at least be glad that he picks up the phone and talks when you call.

Try to tune into your child's contact rhythm and march to his beat:

Brenda, a mom: *I told Keith that I wanted him to call me every week, and then he didn't. So then I was like "Well, I guess you don't need to." And then I realized, well, I don't really need to talk to him every week, and so about every two weeks we talk.*

An important part of the process of your child coming to feel like he's an adult is his having a say in how you two keep in touch. Letting your child set the pace conveys respect and trust.

Another good change assister trick is assuming that no news is good news:

Martin, a dad: *When we don't hear from her, we know that things are very good, that she's very happy and very busy. When she needs a parental injection, she'll call.*

> **It's impossible to predict how your child will respond to the start of college. She might be homesick and call you all the time until she feels settled. She might get swept away in the excitement and barely talk to you until winter break. Or her need to talk might vary from week to week, month to month.**

The Drawbacks to Talking Often The law of diminishing returns applies to frequency of contact. A certain amount is really nice, keeps the connection feeling fresh and up-to-date. Too much, however, and you lose that peak of mutual interest and excitement; the conversation goes stale: "If you call too much the person is going to say, 'Wow, I don't have anything to say.' You run out of topics," one student said.

Do you watch the daily local news on TV at night? Well, can't that get kind of dull and depressing? It dredges up whatever it can to keep you entertained. But buy the Sunday newspaper, and it gives you the best of what the week had to offer. Maybe if you or your child is a David Letterman type who's entertaining enough to have your own nighttime program daily, then frequent contact would work for you both; but even Letterman has a host of writers working for him. You just don't want to be sharing with your child what you did today, and every day—that's for your close friends and romantic partner; the same goes for your child.

Also, your child doesn't want to think that you're waiting by the phone for his call, but he does like to hear excitement in your voice when you and he do touch base:

Max, a student: *When I do call my dad, he's very excited. If I called him more often, he probably wouldn't be as excited or as interested; there wouldn't be as much to talk about.*

Having a Regularly Scheduled Check-in Time A schedule that seems to work well for many families is the once-a-week check-in that leaves open the possibility of "simply feel like it" calls in between. Sunday evening is such a popular time that I'm surprised the phone lines don't jam. In change assister families, Sunday evening is often the anticipated touch-base time, but it's not ironclad; sometimes people have alternative plans. Perhaps the student has homework to prepare or wants to go see a movie with a friend? No problem. If the parents can't reach their child, they leave a message and wait for her to catch up with them later in the week.

In change resister families, however, failure to connect at the designated time makes parents feel anxious:

Adam, a student: *If I don't see my mom on the weekend, she calls every Sunday night at the appointed time. If I'm not there, she's nagging me for months.*

Even just one incidence of disconnection can unleash all your deepest fears about losing your child to university life or even worse, you might imagine that your child has been attacked and is lying wounded somewhere.

Thus, this plan becomes a set-up for disappointment. What can you do? Visualize the reality of your child's busy college living. One of the defining qualities of campus life is spontaneity. Your child is adapting well if he's able to go with the flow of college that sweeps him up carrying him to the dining hall, the library, the pizza place, class, home for a nap, out to a party.

If you're a parent who has high expectations and are easily disappointed, then avoid disaster—make the calling more free-form. Families in the next section talk about how this works well for them.

Having a regularly appointed weekly check-in time only works well if parents can stay calm when it turns out that their child is unavailable.

Calling When They Have Something to Say Plenty of loving families take a more casual approach to staying in touch:

Roy, a student: *If my dad needs to tell me something, he calls me. If I need something, I call him. We call each other on a need-to-know basis. Rarely do I call and say, "How ya doing?" I probably would do that more if I didn't call so much otherwise. Usually every week there's some sort of reason to call. We make plans for me to borrow the car. When I sprained my ankle and he was worried how I was, he called to make sure I was okay. Those kind of things.*

One situation in which the need-to-know flow fails is when parents call because they feel the need to know their child's whereabouts:

Samantha, a student: *It's my first time away from home and my parents would call at two o'clock, three o'clock in the morning, and they'd leave messages on my answering machine, "Where are you?" At first I didn't know what to tell them. Then, finally I just broke it down to them, "Look, I go out." They ask where, and I'll be like "Well, I was at this bar last night."*

You want to demonstrate as much confidence and trust in your child as you possibly can, because the more you show, the more she's likely to live up to it. Besides, your calling won't change her behavior; if anything, it might antagonize her to stay out even later than she normally would, fig-uring that you'd be asleep by 4:00 A.M. It's also a sure-fire way to destroy the warmth you want to establish with your child, as well as to develop serious sleep deprivation.

There's another common change resister trap embedded in the need-to-know calling plan. When a child calls mainly when he needs something, change resisters are prone to think, "My child is calling me because he wants me to do something for him, not because he wants to talk to me." The assumption is made that you as a person don't count for much. But this isn't how your child is feeling. If your child genuinely wasn't inter-ested in talking to you, he would find a way to not need any parental help.

If your child calls mainly when he needs something, you may feel personally discounted. Don't overlook the fact that he could have chosen an alternative route and bypassed you all together; he called at least partly because he loves you.

Humor is a terrific tension diffuser. A pair of change assister parents recorded the following phone message after their last child left home: "You've reached the Jones residence. If you are one of the Jones's children and you need emotional support, press one; financial assistance, press two; disaster relief, press three."

Other problems arise when you assume that your child has received your phone message, but there are even odds that he hasn't. College roommates, no matter how friendly and accommodating they may sound on the phone, are often not the most reliable people on the planet. Even if you leave a message on a machine or voice mail system, the information is often filtered through the roommate. The not knowing can be incredibly frustrating. Unfortunately, you don't have much choice other than to accept the un-certainty of the situation. Do a periodic spot-check to find out if messages are getting through. Harassing the roommates with multiple calls—while a tempting option—won't get you anywhere, except maybe on eternal hold.

If you're unhappy that you're falling into the pattern in which you and your child call each other on a need basis, then consider the possibility that your child might like it even less than you do:

Tabitha, a student: Usually I'm the one who calls. And sometimes I call to see what's up, but usually I call because I need something. I would like it if my mom called me more just to see how I'm doing.

That's the funny thing about communication; it often goes awry. Two people are participating in a certain type of interaction that neither likes but thinks the other does, so they continue. Experiment with a "Hello, how are you?" call a few times and see what happens.

Play the Length of the Call by Ear Prepare yourself for the possibility that the time you call is not always going to be the best time. If your child is awkward upon answering the phone, maybe he's entertaining a special someone in his room but can't say so. Maybe his roommate has been teasing him that he's a mamma's boy. Maybe a prospective freshman is taking a tour of his room. You have no idea; hide your curiosity, respect his privacy, and plan to talk another time:

Paul, a student: The other night I was working on this huge paper and my computer crashed, and I hadn't saved anything; I was a bitter person—not very happy. My dad called just at that time and it was irritating because he was like "What are you working on?" and I was like "Everything just crashed." And he asked, "Well, what's the topic of the paper?" and he was asking all these details about it. And I was just like "Leave me alone, I'm busy."

What would you have done in this situation? An empathic tone can work wonders when your child is stressed out: Saying, "Is there anything I can do to help?" along with, "Good luck. I'll catch you at a better time," would certainly be a comforting response. Imagine how you would feel if you were at work and had either a deadline or crisis to contend with, and the phone rings.

Change assister parents aren't always met with an enthusiastic welcome; they just know when to cut their losses and try again some other time. The length of each call is unpredictable because it changes along with life's circumstances:

Roy, a student: *When we talk on the phone, I don't feel obliged to talk very long. If I want, I'll talk one, maybe two hours, sometimes I'll just say this happened blah, blah, blah—five minutes.*

It's best not to make getting off the phone a tug of war:

Beverly, a student: *She calls me up all the time just to talk, and has a hard time when I say. "Well Mom, I have to go study." And she'll say, "I understand. I understand." Then she'll keep talking for like five more minutes, and I'll be all, "Mom, I have to go now." And she'll be all, "Okay."*

The fewer expectations you put on your child, the more she'll want to talk for longer periods. If she gets the feeling that she's always disappointing you—or that if she gives you more time on one call, then you'll expect more the next time—she may start dodging calls.

The Student Staying in Touch with All Family Members When students are away from home, they like to have contact with everybody in the family. While family conference calling can be nice, also create occasional opportunities for students to touch base with family members individually. When a family falls into a pattern in which the child talks mainly to one parent who relays all the information, the parent who's left out can feel hurt:

Rebecca, a student: *When I call, I'll always ask for my mom. When I get off the phone I always wonder how that makes my dad feel. Maybe he's a little hurt, but I really don't think he thinks about it or that it's a real issue with him.* **James, her father:** *There is very little contact between us, she chooses to talk to her mother whenever she can. If I answer the phone, she'll say, "Is Mom there?" Almost all of the contact is between her and her mother, and I resent that; I don't think it's right.*

If you feel left out of the conversations, next time your child calls and you answer the phone, say, "Hey, good to hear from you. Let's chat a little." You may hear silence on the other end for a few seconds because it takes time for your child to process something new. Also, you don't have to wait for your child to call; surprise her and phone her at a time you know is good for her. The first few conversations will be awkward, but then you'll both settle into a rhythm. Your child will be glad you broke the isolation pattern.

Staying in touch with all family members can be complicated when both parents don't live together, even more so when divorced parents have remarried so that there are two sets of parents and siblings. Take your cues from your child as to whether or not she wants to speak with parent and step-parent at the same time.

Avoid Mixed Messages While you're trying to decipher the meaning behind your child's calling behavior, he's busy trying to understand the message behind yours. When a parent says to a child, "Call more often," and then "Watch the phone bill," the kid is confused. He's stuck in a damned if you do, damned if you don't situation.

If you wish the calls could be more frequent, but know that they can't be due to the family's financial constraints, then come right out and say this. If you can afford it, the action later in this chapter provides several different ways to make your child calling you as welcoming as possible.

E-Mail, Cell Phones, and Beepers: What Modern Technology Has Done for Parent-Student Communication

How up-to-date are you when it comes to technology? Have you entered the new millennium or are you happy living the old-fashioned way? There's nothing at all wrong with wanting to stick to a low-profile, low-tech life, but after you read this section, you might be eager to change your lifestyle just a tad. Learning to use new technology is as easy as one-two-three. You can master cell phones and beepers within two minutes, and E-mailing in fifteen minutes.

If it's the cost that concerns you, new technology is getting cheaper and cheaper, although cell phone bills can run sky-high very quickly. Basic computers that allow you Internet access are dirt-cheap, especially if you get a cash rebate by signing up for a specific Internet service. If you have the computer already, then you can receive free Internet access through certain service providers (see Appendix).

If, however, high-tech communication is beyond your budget, don't feel badly; all the benefits of having a rejuvenated relationship with your college-aged child will still be just as easily yours. After all, families managed for over a century to reach each other in a low-tech world.

The Benefits of the New Technology Technological advances, especially cell phones and E-mail, add convenience to communication, which is a huge deal when all of you in the family lead hectic lives. For some students, the cell phone is simply a comfort to carry in case an emergency crops up. For others, it provides easy access to parents:

Rachel, a student: I am so rarely at my dorm room. I would say that overall, my cell phone is used for 75 percent of my phone calls and that it accounts for almost 90 percent of calls to my parents or from my parents. It is very convenient to be able to call them from anywhere and I am able to talk to them more often. Otherwise we would always be playing phone tag.

E-mail can be a reliable and easy way of getting a message to your child, arranging practical matters, and passing along chatty updates:

Tommy, a student: For some reason my family always manages to call while I'm studying, or busy, or out. It's so much easier to be able to read and respond to E-mail at 3:00 A.M., if that's when you have free time. It's less intrusive than the phone. Plus, it saves a LOT of money!

You don't need to inform your kid every time you get a haircut; but if you get eight inches cut off, she might like to know. E-mail can also ease the time pressure on your child if you and her other parent are divorced and living separately.

E-mail may also enhance a family's sense of connection:

Fabian, a student: Because you are not doing it in real time, you can take as long as you want to figure out what you want to say. I find that I can relate my emotions and thoughts better on the computer rather than through my voice.

Emily, a student: I find that I communicate with my family much more. It's chipped away a bit of the awkward barrier between parents and their children, at least in my situation. And it's made my parents feel like I'm not as much away than if they didn't hear from me.

Whole new worlds may open up. Maybe you'll end up on your child's "forward" list in which jokes and odd stories that sail through the Net and land on her laptop will be sent your way. Maybe funny information will come to you from other sources that you can screen and pass on to your child. It's nice to share the lighter side of life. Maybe she'll be doing a paper for school, and you just happen to come across relevant websites and send the web addresses her way. Besides, joining the Internet revolution will prove to your child that you can handle the new millennium; she'll worry less about you.

Despite all the benefits of E-mail, the telephone still has the edge when it comes to the personal touch:

Daniel, a student: The voice can convey worlds which E-mail can't. E-mail would make things a lot less intimate and exciting.

E-mail is a supplement to the phone, rather than a substitute.

What to Watch Out For The key is to use these electronic devices as communication aids, not, to quote one student, as "electronic leashes." Beepers in particular seem to have a potentially negative effect; an unanswered attempt at paging a child is capable of triggering a beeper frenzy:

Tonya, a student: When she can't reach me on my normal phone and has something important to say she'll page me, but I usually have my pager buried at the bottom of my bag and don't remember to check it very often. The paging decreases the quality of our contact because when my mom pages me, she pages me repeatedly and it can get rather annoying.

With a beeper, the student has no means of calling you back at that moment, not to mention the fact that you very easily could have caught him at a busy time. The challenge for you is to be complacent with just one page.

With cell phones, students love the convenience of being able to reach parents anytime, but most don't want to be tracked down all the time. Ask your child how much he wants you to call him on his cell. Let him know that he won't hurt your feelings if he makes it a 911 family phone. If he seems unenthusiastic when you call on the cell, call less and don't take it personally; new technologies carry the potential to be intrusive. Remind yourself that people often turn their cell phones off or simply don't answer them. Plus, cell phones are so small, and the connection can be so fuzzy, that people tend to shout into them, rather than talk; they lack privacy and intimacy.

The "use it, don't abuse it" motto holds for your child as well. If your kid is having trouble weaning herself from you, having easy access to you through a cell phone can become a crutch that prevents her from putting more effort into adapting to her new surroundings:

Laurel, a student: I talk to my mom at least once a day. I'm very dependent on my relationship with my mother, so if I have free time and I'm sitting around on the street somewhere, I might call her on my cell, when I usually wouldn't have had the access to do so.

Cell phones give kids an easy way to check in with the parental secure base; the question is, is it too easy? Is this college student spending less time exploring around her than she would without her cell? It's scary to be thrown into a new environment. Yet, keeping her head and mind buried in the phone takes her out of the moment; a lot of college adjustment comes from being open to whatever is happening in the here and now. Of course you don't want to cut the cord, and part of you enjoys all the calls, but you also know that she needs to become more related to her immediate surroundings. You can share all of these feelings with her and plan together on how to gradually alter the situation.

You may be wondering whether or not change resister tendencies can creep their way into E-mails as well. One way is that you might be tempted to, as Heather put it, "always include the usual reminder to do well in school." Or perhaps bombarding your child with messages in an attempt to persuade her to come home for the holidays. The great thing about E-mails is that you can always click on the "send later" option and review the E-mail when you're in a different mood—preferably a more change assister mood—and decide whether or not you want to edit the message or delete it altogether. Letting an E-mail sit in your computer overnight can do wonders.

On average, parents tend to send more E-mails than their kids do; you may send three E-mails for every one that your child sends. As long as he doesn't feel deluged, that's fine. The challenge for you will be to accept this ratio and not take it personally. Try to think of an E-mail as sending an "I'm thinking of you" card.

Snail Mail With high technology on the rise, traditional mail takes a back seat, but never underestimate the power of a letter or care package. Students appreciate the time and thought that goes into a piece of mail. Your child will love being able to hold something concrete from you in his hands, and maybe even display it on a shelf as a reminder of your support. Kids enjoy receiving newspaper and magazine article clippings, cards saying, "Hang in there; you can do it," and especially, care packages:

Jordan, a student: When people go far away from home, they get tons of letters or care packages from their parents, and I never got any of that just 'cause I live so close. You kind of want the camp feeling at first when you go away to college.

Snail mail is a nice way to say, "I'm wishing you well," without demanding a response in return. The action includes specific suggestions for putting together a caring care package.

ACTION
Being Your Child's Secure Base from a Distance

1. **Find the Best Balance.**
   a. You don't have to be a mind reader, just be sensitive to:
   - The tone of your child's voice when you call more or less frequently.
   - The quality of the conversations when you call her versus when she calls you.

- How her needs vary depending on the exam phase, job demands, and social turmoil.

b. Ask your child directly what type of calling plan she prefers. If you suspect that she is trying to avoid hurting your feelings, then say, "I'm strong; if you're trying to protect my feelings, there's no need to." If your child seems to be avoiding you, ask her, "Is there something I'm doing that's making our calls unappealing?" Notice how the ideal approach is giving your child room to criticize you. While you don't need a full body of steel armor to withstand a response, there is a certain toughness required; this is called trying to develop a thick skin for the sake of your child. Keep your strategy flexible to accommodate her changing needs, and establish a precedent of checking in about how it's all going.

2. Read the Contact Objectively.

a. If you're dissatisfied with the amount of contact, ask yourself where your expectations come from. Desire? Past experience? Consider every possible way that you could not take the lack of contact personally and focus on those, e.g., her personality and current life phase.

b. Is your child being swept away by the excitement of school? Recall a time in your life when you felt carried away by a new experience, and view your child's ability to be in the moment as a positive quality. Take some credit for helping him get to the point where he can do this. Comfort yourself with the thought that life's intense experiences often come in waves that sweep you up, carry you off, and then plop you down again. While your child is on his exciting adventure, why not find new territory to explore yourself? You could go an African safari, check out the arts community in your town, or take up a new sport.

3. Cover the Phone Charges.

The option of having your child itemize the phone bill is cumbersome and intrusive. If you can afford it, arrange it so that he feels like he has a Bat Phone— a line that goes directly to you free of charge. Here are various options:

a. Install an 800 toll-free number just for your children to call in when they're away from home.

b. Establish the expectation that when your child calls, you will hang up and call her right back.

c. Encourage your child to call you collect. Watch out though; this can get expensive.

d. Cover your child's entire phone bill—no questions asked.

4. Putting Together a Caring Care Package.

The key is to make sure that the contents send the message, "Thinking of you," not "Wanting you to eat well and brush your teeth." Balance out the bottle of multi-vitamins with playful and indulgent items. The most enjoyable part is basing the contents on what you know and love about your child. Here are a few ideas to get you started:

- Munchy, delicious study food. Microwavable popcorn isn't a bad start. If you bake, all the better.
- A videotape with several episodes of a show you used to watch together on cable.
- Send his favorite recipe of yours, along with all the nonperishable ingredients.
- A book of cartoons, good jokes, or odd facts that he can use for a study break or to amuse his friends.
- A silly gadget, like a yo-yo or wind-up toy.

Send a few packages over the course of each year and your child will adore you!

Visits—Seeing Your Child Up Close and Personal

To mix a couple of metaphors: Phone calls and E-mails are the bread and butter of parent-student contact, while visits are the icing on the cake. What could be better than to see your child's facial expressions as he talks, smell the gunk he uses in his hair, and take note of his typical sloppy outfit? He's everything you remembered him to be with a tad more maturity.

Visits vary in their meaning depending upon how close to school you live, whether the contact occurs on campus or the home turf, and whether or not it's for a short stretch or the long summer. Most parents would love to see their college-aged children often. This wish is more of a fantasy, especially when kids are attending school miles and miles away. Given the long-distance situation, the winter break and summertime are the best bets. Spring break is often a tossup between a vacation with friends to some tropical or snow-covered locale and family time. As your child moves along through the college years, you may end up with bits and pieces of his longer vacations; work, travel with friends, and campus commitments can all become rivals for your child's time.

Having a child live close by can be a blessing, but it can also feed you material for self-torture, "She's only half an hour away, why can't I see her more?" Assister parents have an answer to this question—"My child's life is hectic and exploding with new possibilities on campus; that's where she belongs." The nagging voice inside a change resister's head, rather than being reassuring, whispers over and over, "My child doesn't love me as much as she used to." This section will help quell your fears and also will help you maximize the enjoyment of the time you do have together, as well as increase the odds that your child will return more often for an infusion of family time.

Readjusting Expectations for the Amount of Contact
Here's why visits home typically aren't as frequent as parents would like.

Social Life What may seem like a small campus event to you can feel like a huge one to your child. A party where his big crush might make an appearance. An event he's been planning with his extracurricular club. A study group where he can benefit from the knowledge of others and socialize—the social component makes grueling tasks more palatable:

Rebecca, a student: I'm expected to go home when my mom calls and asks me, because I feel like it's a duty. I feel a little burdened because I have school and other activities going on with my sorority. A lot of times when I go home, I lose track of my agenda that I follow when I'm at school. I lose time being here with my friends.

When you find yourself thinking, "My child can socialize with her friends round-the-clock at school, how about a little time for me," remind yourself that time spent with friends, just hanging out in the dorm even, helps your child adjust to the school. Think back to a period when you were in school and looked forward to hanging out with friends and dating.

Academic Life When it comes to doing homework and studying for exams, it seems perfectly reasonable to assume that your home would be just as good, if not better, for delving into the books than campus would be. Your child can have her own room, home-cooked meals, and no phone ringing to disturb her—being productive would be a breeze. What could be bad? Well, here's what usually happens:

Heather, a student: I don't get any work done when I go home. Home is really comfortable; I'd plan to study and end up sleeping half of the weekend away. I will sleep all day and watch TV all day, and in my dorm I don't have those distractions. At the dorm, my roommate would study too so that would keep me on my toes. The commuting time alone takes all your energy away— just sitting there. When I stay here at school, I do study a lot on the weekends and get a lot done.

After a few experiences of lugging home armfuls of huge textbooks, and finding that the only result is that they've developed a backache from the load, students learn their lesson. It's incredibly discouraging for a college student to head into a weekend with big studying plans and end up on Monday having gotten nothing done. She'll receive five new assignments and will start feeling out of control. Schoolwork piles up and up and up. Assimilating new information will depend on your child having a grasp of past homework assignments. Your child needs to feel in charge of her study time or else her foundation of competence crumbles.

This description doesn't even include the required access to libraries, review sessions, study buddies, reference resources, and TAs. In the old days, collegiate academics seemed to revolve around a more predictable schedule with midterms clumped together in the actual middle of the term and finals occurring at the end of the semester. Today, there always seems to be a paper due, plus a second or third midterm.

Sure, there are plenty of perks to being a college student: many mornings of sleeping late, summers off, few financial responsibilities. Remember, though, the job of a student never ends—there's always something hanging over your child's head, something she *should* be doing. So when your child says she has a ton of work to do, believe her. Odds are that she's telling the truth and not trying to wheedle her way out of seeing you.

Your home cannot rival a campus library or late-night study group.

Is there anything you can do to make your home environment more conducive to productive studying? Increasing the comforts of home won't work; it's because home *is* so comfortable that studying is her last choice of what to do. I suppose you could get rid of the TV and bring in mattresses made of stone, but clearly that's not the answer. What you can do is enjoy the fact that your home can be your child's safe, comfy haven, and be completely accepting of his expressed need to remain at school.

Coping with Infrequent Visits How do change assisters act on their understanding of college students' hectic lives? They extend an open invitation to their child, implying "This is still your home. You're welcome to come home anytime at your convenience and stay for as long or as short a period as you like." There is absolutely no pressure. Sure these parents have hopes, but they convey their hope as love not expectation.

If their child phones to say that he's made alternative plans for a vacation break, change assister parents don't freak out. Be forewarned that kids do this all the time. Don't feel like you have to try to woo your child with expensive vacation plans that you can't really afford. Your child will cycle in and out of spending vacation time with you. Ask your child if there is anything special he would like to do over a break and try to accommodate, but don't put your life on hold. If he's making other plans, you should too. See this as an opportunity. If there are no kids left at home, then plan a second honeymoon with your spouse or if you're unattached, explore a new country and/or go on a singles trip with a friend.

If it's the holiday rituals that you miss the most, resist the temptation to try to lure your child home. Warnings of "We'll be having a great time. What will you do on campus with everybody gone?" and pleadings of "Your grandma is getting old and is dying to see you" won't get you a smiling face walking in the door. It's a wonderful instinct to want to preserve family traditions; the action includes some tips on how to do this in such a way that you don't impinge on your child's new lifestyle.

If you are separated or divorced, and your child has contact with your ex-spouse, then negotiating visits can be more complicated, and you rarely feel like you have enough time with your child. The action section has special tips for you.

While you can't control when your child does and doesn't come home, you can make the visits home as welcoming as possible using the following tricks of the parenting trade.

Creating a Welcoming Environment

Keeping Your Child's Room as Is Change assister parents do what they can to maintain their child's room as is—a freezing in time of when their child was fully integrated into family life. Your child is aware that life at home has gone on without her, but she still wants to feel like she holds an important place, even if she's not always there to occupy it:

Pamela, a student: My parents leave it up to me to come home; the door is open to me—I have a key. My parents certainly like it when I come home. Our rooms are still our rooms. As soon as we moved out, they didn't make it into a guest room or anything like that; so I could always come back.

When a kid comes home to a house that now lacks his special space, he feels displaced, as if the welcome mat has been pulled out from under his feet:

Joe, a student: It was strange for me to see that life kind of progressed on without me. I mean it's kind of a shock to come home and realize, "Oh, I don't have a room in this house anymore." I was worried that I'd feel like a stranger visiting home if I had to stay in the guest room or something. And it did sort of feel that way.

If you have limited space and siblings are used to performing the "where do I sleep?" shuffle, then a room takeover could be inevitable. If you can wait until at least the first visit home, that would be best. Also, let your college student help the younger sibling make the move—a handing down ritual from the elder to the younger. If it's a matter of storing the family's stuff versus preserving your kid's room, then do an early spring cleaning.

If you're looking forward to using your child's room to house a hobby of yours, then set up a temporary shop that you can tear down easily before your child's visits. Don't hide the fact that you're doing this, but also try to respect the privacy of her things and avoid leaving scraps—signs of your presence—lying around. If you need to do some major furniture moving, then wait until your child visits and rearrange the room together. This could be a defining symbol of how things change and yet stay the same.

Keeping the Amount of Family Strife to a Minimum You don't want to pretend to be the cast from *Father Knows Best* when your child comes home, but you also don't want to let it all hang out:

Matthew, a student: Last semester, I would go home on the weekends, and my mom would be on my sister for something. I would say, "Stop this! That's not what I came home for!" Just basically get them both to shut up. I don't really want conflict when I go home. I want to relax.

It's no surprise that Matthew visits less. While the dorms can be hectic and fraught with tiffs, family strife still causes a great deal more upset for your child. It's not just that your child wants peace and quiet, it's that he cares about you all a lot and it upsets him to see you not getting along. Wanting to see your child more often can be a good incentive for the family to work through the conflict. Plan activities that bring out the best in family relationships—situations in which you laugh together and cooperate. This might mean going out to see a romantic comedy film, or staying home and playing Pictionary.

Respecting Your Child's Need for Space and Privacy Your child's been away and is coming home for a visit; you imagine high-quality time spent chatting in the kitchen, going to your favorite places together, renting movies you've both been wanting to see. Yet, somehow it never quite turns into your vision of togetherness. Sure, your child probably isn't cooped up in her room doing all that productive studying she had planned to do, but she's also not necessarily so available. Recall why students said that studying at home was hard and you'll get the picture that this father describes: "He sleeps in until 2:00 P.M., and then comes in and watches TV all day."

If your child is awake and not being hypnotized by the TV, then he might be on the phone with college pals or meeting up with old friends from the neighborhood. That dinner you made of all his favorite foods turns into a meal on the fly as he runs out the door.

College students' lives are so crazy that even when they come home every weekend, their parents still hardly see them. Neal, for example, comes home on weekends to work his job from Friday night through Saturday and then hangs out with his girlfriend and neighborhood friends who are attending the community college. He barely sees his parents. Also, many parents of commuter students complain that they rarely spend any quality time with their children, let alone catch a glimpse of them; "He might as well be living at school for all the time I see him."

When your child is so close, yet so far, you're left feeling disappointed and unappreciated. What can you do? First, here's an example of what to avoid doing:

Samantha, a student: I think sometimes that I should just be able to go in my room, shut the door, and not be bothered until I come out. My mom and I disagree about this. I'll stay in the room for an hour or two. And like clockwork, she always comes in the first half an hour and says, "How are you?" She checks up on me. And then comes in a half an hour later, "Oh well, I just thought you might want to know . . ."—something totally meaningless, off the top of her head, just to check up on me. She takes my being in my room really personally. She turns it into a family issue, especially since I've gone off to school. She says, "We're still your family. We'll always be here for you." Yes, I know that, but I want time to myself. She can't understand that because she takes it as a personal attack against her, which makes it hard.

An important part of the picture that this mother fails to take note of is that one of the potential advantages of home over the dorm is privacy.

Giving your child some space and quiet will do wonders for her wanting to return.

Lowering your expectations for how much time you and your child will spend together when she visits will leave you open for pleasant surprises.

The less you pressure her to stand still and talk, the more likely she will want to do it. Lower your expectations for quantity of contact, but hold onto hope. When you actually do get a chance to catch up, the quality of the conversation can take on all sorts of new dimensions now that your child is out in the world.

Decide which family events you most want your child to participate in and ask her ahead of time what might be the best time to schedule it. Think about what your child loves to do that she has less access to on campus. If she is anything like the rest of America's college population, being fed well and being taken shopping for her favorite clothes or gadgets would be quite high on her wish list.

Include Your Child's Friends Change assisters may not like the following statement, but they accept it: A mother said, "As the kids are growing older, they have the tendency to be more with their friends." As discussed earlier, kids will be reluctant to leave their friends on campus. When they do come home, they might spend an inordinate amount of time on the phone.

Then there are students who remain close to friends who have stayed around the neighborhood. Your child might come home to visit, change clothes, and run out the door to meet friends. Between time going out and phone calls, there's always downtime. The hope is that *you'll* actually be available when that time occurs.

The danger is that you might start resenting your child for seeming to choose friends over you, as if they're his future and you're just his past. Assure yourself that there is plenty of room for all of you in your child's life. Rejoice in the fact that he can make good friends; this is age-appropriate and means that he's adjusting well to life as a young adult.

Apply the philosophy, "If you can't beat 'em, join 'em." Expand the family welcome circle to include your child's friends from home and from school. Invite them for dinner, to spend the weekend, or even away with you for a family trip. This can be fun, and gives you access to a side of your child you might not have otherwise—it lets you into her world. Plus, you'll probably see your child more. Not every kid likes the communal option, but if she's up to it, see where it leads you both.

Allowing for Increased Independence in Terms of House Rules Your kid is not used to having anyone around who cares where he is all the time. You're not used to having somebody extra to keep track of and worry about. He's used to throwing all of his things around the dorm room and having the food hall staff clean his dishes. You're used to having the den the way you left it and fewer dishes to tend to. Adjustments will need to be made; the question is how will this play itself out? There's a fair amount of retraining that has to go on for both parties, and this can take some time.

Everybody is bound to forget their new role in the beginning and revert to old habits. As a parent, it's natural that your tendency will be to fall back on either the new habits formed after your child left, or to regress to the old pre-college house rules. For your child, it makes sense that she would tend to act as she has been at school; freedom is a fun habit, and can easily become addictive. Change assister parents see the conflict for what it is—a clash of habits. As a change resister parent, however, every area of disagreement with your child feels painful—like a personal affront.

The action later in this section has a few tips on how all families can return the home to a comfort zone. Of course, by the time you've completely renegotiated and reconfigured a set of standards that works well for everybody, your child is likely to be on her way back to school again. Don't fret; it will take you less time to get back to this comfortable place the next time she returns.

Problem-solving together with your child will go a long way. The fact that she knows she has a voice in how she functions in the family will be part of the force driving her back home. It's exciting to gain increments of autonomy within the arena that has meant the most to her—her family.

The more your house rules resemble the freedom of the dorms, the happier your child will be to visit.

Visiting Campus

Change Assisters and Resisters
Your child has her own pad. You're probably subsidizing her ability to live independently from you, but this is still a big deal for her. So she's sharing it with several other people and it's not the most beautiful of living quarters, but it's now her second home. Change assister parents seem to instinctively understand the sanctity of the dorm room:

Pamela, a student: My parents do not want to infringe on my place at school. They would not come over here without my desiring that. I think it's appropriate that they come here when it's convenient for me. And when they have reason to come or when they are in the area, they make an effort to come see me; I think that's good.

What's wrong with the following picture?

Madeline, a student: I come home for Sunday night dinner, and hang out there. But my mom comes down on Tuesday night and Thursday night just to see if I'm home. I'd like to have a little more privacy. I mean, she has a key to the place, which kinda sucks. It makes me feel uncomfortable that she's always coming down and visiting me.

While few change resister parents get this carried away, it can happen. Remember that your child is itching to experience whatever independence he has just gained. If he's living in a dorm, then he still has to show his school identification when he comes in, follow the guidelines for what he can and can't do to decorate his room, and sign in and out any visitors. Popping in unexpectedly and unannounced equals pressure. Calling ahead of time with zero expectations is best.

Overindulging in visits to the campus not only could make you unpopular with your child, but it could also make your child unpopular with her peers. Even worse than getting a reputation for running home to Mother is one for having your mother run to you all the time. Space out the visits and let your child miss you. Some kids prefer having the majority of the visits take place at home. Ask your child what her preference is and try to respect it.

If you're curious to see your child's place and he hasn't yet invited you over, he might be thinking, "Why would anyone want to see my ugly dorm room?" Dorms are not known for their appealing aesthetics. He can't quite envision you using the co-ed bathrooms comfortably and, quite frankly, might be embarrassed for you to see the messy state of his affairs, not to mention his supermodel pinups on the wall. Why not try simply saying, "I'd love to see your 'second home'—and I'll close my eyes to whatever mess there may be."

When you visit, your kid might feel torn between seeing his friends and seeing you. You can try making the choice easier by offering to include his friends in your activities. Consider if you can afford to feed and entertain a larger group. Don't extend an invitation directly unless you know for certain that your child does want to share you. There are exceptions; if it's a romantic partner and the two are inseparable, then go ahead and invite.

Attending Events at the College

Parents weekend usually occurs sometime within your child's first semester. By then, hopefully she's had a chance to do some settling in and is ready to receive visitors. The university doesn't want parents visiting when homesickness is still at its height; this is the same principle that sleepaway camps follow—they don't want kids stowing away on the back floors of their parents' cars to make a getaway.

If your child feels ready for a parental visit at the officially designated time, then this could be a great opportunity to see where he lives. Be prepared for the possibility that while you're itching to spend time in his world, your child might be yearning for you to whisk him away from there. Sneak your peek and give him a break from college life if that's what he desires. Your child is still running the show. If your child needs independent time during your stay, consider hooking up with his roommate's parents and going out on the town together.

It could be fun for you and your child to attend college sporting events and root for the home team together. There's only one catch: Some college students find that the games are an excellent way for them to bond with other students. "But my child doesn't even like watching sports!" you might say. It doesn't really matter. The university songs sung in unison at the games, that great feeling when you win, and the parties before, during, and after the game all create camaraderie. Perhaps the football games are peer time, but the basketball games are wide open for family fun—ask her. If your child is an athlete herself, or an actor, dancer, or musician, then you could attend her performance events.

Sororities and fraternities often host events that include parents. It depends on the house and, of course, on whether or not your kid is into parent-child events. Sometimes there are even official roles for parents:

Jane, a mom: When she got involved with the sorority, then I got involved with the mother's club. I helped decorate for Christmas and did things like that. Now I'm the president of the mother's club.

Traditions that revolve around the campus can be comforting to you and your child, and give you both something to look forward to. If the college doesn't provide rituals for you and your child to enjoy together, then consider creating your own:

Heather, a student: When my mom comes up here, we like walking down the main avenue with all the shops. There's this one antique store that we love, and we go there every time she comes here. It's like our spot.

Go out and have fun and see if the "spot" hits: a local billiards hall where you can shoot some pool; a movie house that shows the old movies that you both love; a museum with the type of art you both admire; or a local theatre company that produces the offbeat comedies that crack you both up. If all else fails, there are always the fail-safe options to fall back on—eating and shopping.

Rose, a mother: If we're going to be over there, we'll call Neal and see if he wants to go eat. Food is a big thing. It doesn't really matter what the food is, it seems. Food is love, right?

The campus provides a variety of new, fun activities for you and your child to share, assuming that your child is game.

Issues that Crop Up When Your Child Lives Nearby

If your child lives within an hour travel distance, then she might visit more in the beginning and then less so when her homesickness wears off and she settles in. Or, she might not visit at all until winter vacation.

If your child is coming home every weekend, then you probably realize that this is not necessarily the smoothest of transitions. You can try to gently nudge him out of the nest, by asking if there are any on-campus clubs he might like or any fun events taking place over the weekend; but clearly you shouldn't kick him out of the house. It is crucial that you examine whether or not you're giving any "I need you here" messages. Even if your child says she's not comfortable at school, there may be more to the story than meets the eye; she may be trying to comfort you.

Amenities of Home A student who lives nearby may be thrilled to take advantage of the comforts of home from time to time—laundry facilities, a well-stocked fridge, home-cooked meals, tender loving care when she's ill. Your child can have the best of both worlds:

Stanley, a dad: Max just drives over here. He's got a key and anytime he wants to come over, sleep over, anything, wash his clothes, he can. He knows this is his house too. He comes and he usually hits the refrigerator first, uses the phone, whatever. When he needs a good night sleep, needs to get away from dorm life, it's a good inner change.

Change assister parents relish in the pleasure that comes from giving their child the comforts of home. As a change resister, however, you're more likely to feel unappreciated:

Maxine, a mom: Sometimes he comes home to eat or do laundry, and it's not necessarily just to see his father or me. I almost think it's a practical issue more than anything else.

Joe, Maxine's son: *I'd come home every weekend, but then I think my mom thought, "Oh, you're just using this house as a hotel, coming back to sleep here and eat here and then you leave." Sometimes she would say that and she was angry.*

If you're feeling taken for granted or used, then remind yourself: With the time it takes your kid to pack laundry and travel back and forth, he could have gotten his clothes cleaned in the dorms. By coming home for any reason he is engaging in a relationship with you, despite the fact that this isn't the explicit purpose. Whatever pressure you're feeling to "let go" of your child, he's feeling pressure "not to run home to Mother." Despite that, he comes home.

Another possibility is that you feel like you're a pickup and delivery service:

Jane, a mom: *It's always, "I need more money, Mom. I need to be picked up. The car is banged up. What am I gonna do with it?" I have to be constantly changing my schedule to fit hers. We don't mind, but when she says, "Mom, I need to be picked up today," and if I have twenty patients scheduled for that day, it kind of bothers me. And she does this at the eleventh hour. She could have easily let me know three days ahead. But this way I'm left feeling frustrated because I can't do it for her; and at the same time I tell myself, why should I let my patients down for a child who's irresponsible?*

If your child makes too many practical demands on you, set your limits. You will be a good role model for her in her own life. Don't cut off the lifeline, but let her know what you reasonably can and can't do. You love her and want to help, but you need to fulfill your other interests and obligations as well. Work out a plan together.

ACTION
Making the Most Out of Visits

1. **More Ways to Make Home as Appealing as Possible.**
   a. Know what your hometown has to offer and play that up. For example, if you live in a big city, then research the musicians who will be performing,

the exhibits at the art museums, new theatre offerings—anything he can't get at school—and send him the information.

b. Help your kid spice up the long vacations. Summers, or even winter breaks, at home can be long stretches of time. While some kids enjoy extended veg-out periods, others get antsy without something to do. If your kid is the restless type, then suggest that she look into an internship with college alumni who work nearby, summer classes at a local college for credit, a fun artsy class in music, painting, writing, or dance, or a job that introduces her to the day-to-day workings of a career. Planning a family trip to break up the time can't hurt either.

2. Renegotiate the Rules of the House.

Keep in mind that it's advisable to give him freedom comparable to what he'd have living on his own with a roommate. Otherwise, you risk having him bolt.

a. Acknowledge that you have to make room for his increasing maturity and independence, and he needs to understand you've restructured a bit since he left. If you two tend to get stuck on opposing sides, try an exercise in which you each describe the situation from the other person's point of view; on each issue, you describe his needs, and he describes yours.

b. Experiment with your child not having a curfew. To help you worry less, consider listening to National Public Radio, reading a good book, or wearing earplugs so that you can't hear when he comes home. If this doesn't work, then tell your child your dilemma: "I trust you, but I still worry. What can we do?" Hopefully, he'll offer some kind of calling plan in which he offers to call you if he's not going to be home by, say, 3:00 A.M. Be forewarned that this plan will have loopholes—it won't always be easy for him to call. If your child is getting around by car and you're concerned about drunk driving, then ask him what his plans are for keeping himself safe.

c. For household chores, it might be to your advantage to let him crash at home for the weekend with few responsibilities. A little pampering will make home all the more appealing. Communicate expectations that he pick up after himself. For longer stays, devise a plan together. It's important to make your specific wishes explicit so that you don't set up the situation in which your child has two choices: reading your mind or disappointing you.

d. If you are separated or divorced, then see if you and your ex can arrange to institute similar house rules. Consistency will be comforting for your child.

3. Devise Ways to Celebrate the Holidays Long-Distance.

a. Send your child a holiday care package that includes mementos, such as items from the traditional table setting, music you usually play, photos of past gatherings, food or recipes, the board game you play after the meal. Give the message, "We miss you, but it's OK that you're not here. Hope you have a good one." The unintentional effect might be that your child becomes nostalgic and returns for the next event.

b. Re-create the holiday when your child is home. That wonderful Thanksgiving dinner—who says that you can't have it in January? Ask your child what he missed most over the holidays he was away for, and re-celebrate—light a menorah and play dreidel, have an Easter egg hunt, sing holiday songs. It will feel weird at first, but you could easily get used to having more celebration in your life.

4. Overcome the Difficulties of Negotiating Contact When You Are Divorced or Separated.

a. As if it wasn't hard enough devising a visitation schedule with your ex-spouse *before* your child went off to college, now you have even less time to divide up. Give your child space to make her own decisions, and try not to resent the choices she makes. What usually happens is that the child leans toward preserving the previous balance. If this means that one parent is consistently left out of the loop, then let your child know that she needs to create a better balance. Remember, neighborhood friends' schedules also factor into her decisions. If your child desires more time with you than she is able to give, consider offering to visit her more often on campus.

b. If the divorce was particularly bitter, with many feelings left unresolved, then make sure that your child doesn't get caught in the crossfire. The preferable route might be to work out a schedule with your ex that takes into account your child's wishes. Even if the last thing you feel like is your ex's ally, you need to act as one.

c. For special events on campus, visit on alternating occasions. Everybody should be there for graduation to show their love, support, and admiration. Of course if everyone gets along famously, then ignore the previous advice and just function as one big, happy not-together family.

d. Be sympathetic to your child's plight. The fact that she knows you respect how difficult it is for her to try to please everybody will, in and of itself, ease her burden. Also, don't for a second feel guilty for having contributed to the difficulties; by ending your marriage, you saved both you and your child from future grief. Children are better off with happier parents who are no longer together than ones who are stuck in an unhappy union.

e. Be on the lookout for the fact that as a single parent, you may be more likely to pull for excessive closeness. Without a spouse around, you and your child could easily have formed an extra close-knit bond, so you miss her terribly.

Your Child's Sharing of Personal Information

College Students Demonstrate a Wide Range of Styles

As a parent you're probably very tuned into how much your child does and doesn't open up to you about her personal life. College kids run the gamut from sharing practically nothing to spilling their guts. Some kids share information about their social lives, but are closed-lipped when it comes to academics, while others are the exact opposite. Some call on their parents mostly when they're hurting and want support; in these cases the parents wind up thinking that their kids are always in a crisis. While other students prefer talking to parents mainly when they're feeling happy, so parents aren't quite sure what to think.

Why so much variation? First of all, some kids just happen to be private and noncommunicative about their emotions in general:

Keith, a student: *I really don't share many feelings with people at all. I'm pretty outgoing and talkative, but I usually don't share a lot of my emotions. I'm not willing to express my personal life. I'm a very private person. Maybe it'd be nicer if I could reveal myself, but I'm just not like that.*

Second of all, many kids have learned to adjust what they tell their parents based on the reactions they get. If talking about their romantic lives leads to tension, then they're likely to keep this knowledge to themselves. If the topic of career goals leads to arguments, then they'll steer the conversation clear of the subject. This is the basic behavioral psychology principle of negative reinforcement in action: If something your child talks about repeatedly elicits a negative response, then she will stop sharing that type of information. You don't have to always agree with your child, simply be careful to express an opposing opinion in an agreeable manner that leaves her room to make her own decisions.

The more open-minded you are, the more personal information your child is likely to share.

Don't worry if you don't have all the answers or you feel like you don't know enough about what kids go through these days. Just expressing parental love is often all that your child needs:

Max, a student: I did have some problems—girl trouble. I was pretty busted up over it and that's actually when I started my closer relationship with my dad 'cause I couldn't believe that he hugged me and told me he loved me. And that was probably the most overwhelming thing I've felt from him. That in part made me feel good and helped me get back in the swing of things.

Lending an Ear without Expectations
When parents are open to receiving information, yet refrain from putting out too many feelers, they reap the rewards:

Francesca, a mom: She's free to share with us and I think she does it because we don't require it or expect it; we don't pry or probe or judge. She's free to come to us, but she also knows that she could go to anyone else. In fact, between brother and sister, they solve a lot of their problems without coming to us parents.

David, the dad: Also, I think it's easier for her to turn to people who are nearby—her roommates and friends. She hears about other options, other ways to handle things; and this is good because her parents might be biased.

Thomas Evans gave the ultimate secure base line: "If my daughter has a need to tell us, then I have a need to listen."

Some kids are most responsive when a parent communicates a willingness to listen, but doesn't actually ask the initial questions:

Max, a student: *The only way we'll talk about it is if I talk about it. My dad will never ask me to talk about something. He'll always let me start it off. Because if I don't start it off, I won't talk about it. I end up sharing quite a bit.*

Some kids liked to be asked about how certain areas of their lives are going, but others don't. Which category does your child fall into?

Sometimes a child shares too much—a potential sign that she's not able to move on and form close friendships. In this case, a change assister parent will try to gently wean the student from his emotional dependence. A change resister parent, on the other hand, might interpret the sharing as affection, as opposed to a trouble sign, and thus, encourage the high level of sharing.

The Change Resister Traps As a change resister parent, you probably have a deep desire to know what is in your child's heart, yet unintentionally discourage him from opening up:

Jennifer, a student: *My mom will say something like, "What's up with so and so . . ." I could talk for five minutes or however long, but when she asks the same thing again and I just talked about the person, it's because she wants to know more. Then I want to stop. I don't mind talking about it, but just accept what I do say; I want her to stop trying to dig, dig, dig.*

If this sounds like you at all, don't be too hard on yourself. You love your child, are interested in her life, and want to help anyway you can. However, backing off is your best bet. Keep in mind that even subtle reactions, like a particular gesture, tone of voice, or facial expression, can be enough of a deterrent.

If you're not careful about the messages you send, you might end up receiving an automatic, "I'm fine," or a dispassionate accounting of how your child spends her time:

Madeline, a student: *If I stopped telling her all the little details in my life she'd probably think that something was wrong with me, that I was backing off and I didn't want to be close to her anymore. I tell her things, but I don't get that personal with her. I let her know what I do, when I do it, who I was with, how much fun it was, but I don't let her know what it was really like. Unless I'm really upset about something or extremely happy about something, I'll just keep the personal things and my feelings to myself.*

Another way that you might inadvertently cause your child to share less is if you hold an idealized view of her that doesn't match who she really is. For example, if you cling to an unrealistic picture of your child, such as that she doesn't go out and party, when actually she does, then she will start editing what she tells you in order to live up to your idealized vision. Let her know that you realize how challenging collegiate academics and social life can be. If she knows that you don't expect her to be perfect, she'll feel freer to express her struggles. Everybody has strengths and weaknesses; see her for who she is and your reward will be that you'll learn more about her.

You Might See Changes in Sharing as Your Child Matures When your child leaves for college, the physical distance may provide enough emotional space that she feels safe to share in ways that she hasn't before. If you don't love what she has to say, she won't have to see your disapproving face when she hangs up the phone. Now that your child is out in the world, she may gain an appreciation for your life experience and what you have to offer as an advisor. You may also be the perfect sounding board against which she can find out how her developing views of the world hold up.

While your child may be expressing more of her feelings and opinions in new arenas, she may also be sharing a little less in others—namely in the realms of romance and night life. It's appropriate that she not call you when she has temporarily misplaced her diaphragm or is battling a hangover. Part of growing up is putting some boundaries around one's private life.

Change assisters are pleased when their kids have friends at school to turn to for immediate assistance. As a change resister parent, you may wish that you could still be your child's main confidant. This tendency is exacerbated by the American myth that the ultimate parental achieve-ment and reward is having your child be your best friend, so that the shar-ing of personal information flows both ways:

Elaine, a mom: I depend on my son Adam for help with emotional stress. I talk to him freely and he supports me a lot. He's a good listener; even though he's young, I know he's mature. He's been taking some courses in psychology. He's very objective and he comes up with good ideas. I really appreciate that he tells me what to do.

It becomes extra tempting to elevate your child to the status of confi-dant at the time of the college transition because he appears to be so grown up, giving you the illusion that he's somewhat of a peer; or even an expert due to one psychology course. Plus, your conflict may be with your spouse or other kids, and of course, your college-aged child is very familiar with the family dynamics. But if the college student is caught be-tween both parents or between his parents and his sibling, he's in a no-win situation. Keep in mind that promoting close sibling relationships among your children is by far one of the greatest gifts that you can pos-sibly give them. Solid, strong sibling relationships can support your chil-dren through the years.

Not only are you still way ahead of your child when it comes to life experience, but also college students stumble under the weight of their parents' problems. Change assister parents seem to know this instinctively:

Brenda, a mom: I like to deal with problems myself and I think my son should not be involved. His job is to fulfill his study in college. My husband and I should try to provide an environment in which our problems don't affect him because it's not good for him if they do. When a person has too many things in his mind, his concentration and everything is affected.

Granted, when you confide in your child she's temporarily flattered be-cause you're complimenting her maturity. What you both don't realize is that she's being set up to fail. As one of the founding fathers of family therapy, Dr. Salvador Minuchin, asserts, you can't rescue your own par-ents, even if you're a trained family therapist.

Simply sharing your personal woes can be detrimental. As the parent, it's your role to reassure your child that one way or another, everything is going to be all right. You told your child that when he was afraid of the dark. You told him that on his first day of nursery school. It's your job to tell him now that he's going off to college. By creating a situation in which your child says to you, "Don't worry, everything will be fine," you render powerless the reassurances you give him. He needs to feel you as the secure base underneath him; otherwise, the world can start to seem like a dangerous place. He needs to still look up to you, not across at you. Spread the word: The genuine quintessential gratification of parenting isn't being your child's best friend—it's watching him flourish. After reading the next section, you may be able to rejoice in the fact that it's not optimal for you and your child to be bosom pals.

It's an American myth that the most satisfying relationship between college-aged kids and their parents is to be best friends.

When Learning a Little Less Is a Blessing in Disguise It's quite possible that underneath your deep desire to hear about your child's personal life, there's an even deeper sense of ambivalence:

Felicia, a mom: I like to hear about Roy's personal life, but sometimes I'm afraid to hear about some of the painful experiences because it makes me feel bad. Sometimes I feel worse than he does. He goes through a breakup with a girlfriend; I'm all worried about him and then somehow he works through it and he's off thinking about something else not worrying about it, while I'm still worried about it.

Parents were given bleeding hearts for the purpose of protecting their kids from further harm. Now that your child is out of the nest, you can't wrap your wings around him, but you can still help out. If your child tends to share a little less about the ups and downs, then this might not be such a bad thing, especially since college is such an erratic time: Moods shift every other hour depending on how well an exam goes, on whether or not a crush is returned or unrequited, and how much conflict there is with a roommate. One week he's loving it at school and feeling on top of the world, the next he's feeling miserable and wants to come home—for good:

Arlene, a mom: *Our daughter is very emotional and tends to be high-strung, very volatile, and outspoken. She expresses her positive and negative feelings. Sometimes I wish she didn't tell us quite as much, that she kept a little more to herself. Sometimes she's just sounding it out and using us as a sounding board. Other times she'll say things like "I'm dropping out of school." And then the next thing you know she's taking the examination for entrance into medical school.*

If you do want your child to share more, here are a few suggestions.

ACTION
Maximizing Chances that Your Child Will Share Information with You

1. Asking Questions Can Show Concern; It's All a Matter of How You Ask.

    a. It's always safe to start with a general, "How's it going?" and see what follows. Then there are questions of the specific, yet general variety, "How's school going? Everything in the dorm? Your professors?" Space out the questions so that your child doesn't experience you as the grand inquisitor. You might find that even if your child doesn't answer your question in the moment, he will some other time. But if you keep asking, then he won't. Or he will divulge in an exasperated way and then subsequently avoid you. Appreciate whatever information is sent your way. Find your own style of inquiry that falls somewhere in between an investigative reporter interviewing for *60 Minutes* and your local grocer asking how you're doing today.

    b. Follow up on information your child gave you previously. If he says he has an exam coming up that he is particularly nervous about, then afterwards, ask him how it went. Tone here is everything. There's the anxious parental inquiry, "How'd you do?" Then there's the empathic approach, "Just calling to say congratulations on finishing and to find out how grueling it was."

c. Keep in mind that despite your child's hectic life, the college days full of studies and hanging out with friends can blend into each other without anything dramatic actually occurring; often no news *really* is good news.

2. Passionate Debates Can Be Productive.

If you find that discussions about everybody's life quickly digress into arguments over moral principles and political policies, rather than view this as a challenge to your authority, see it as your child flexing her new intellectual muscles. Be flattered that she trusts you enough to test out her views on you. College is about figuring out what one believes. Sometimes she has to try on new views before discarding them. Take her seriously, but not so seriously that you get blue in the face from the debate.

To Students

1. If You're Feeling Homesick, Know That This Is Normal.

You have a variety of options for coping:

a. Use your parents as a secure base, while you make efforts to be more connected to your surroundings.

b. Seek out people at school that you know from your hometown, even if they weren't your closest friends.

c. Join an extracurricular group by reconnecting with an activity you used to adore or trying something totally new.

d. Rent your favorite movie or one that is filmed in your hometown. While you watch, chow down on your favorite food from home.

e. Talk to your RA or roommate about missing home. Many people around you are homesick even if they don't seem to be.

2. Let Your Parents Know How You Would Like the Flow to Go.

Be honest with yourself. Do you like it when they call or not? Do you prefer calling them but don't want the burden of having to reach them at a specific time? Maybe you like having a regular check-in time. Just because you feel the need to touch base with your parents doesn't mean that you're not an increasingly independent, maturing young adult. Or just because they're not the main thing on your mind doesn't mean that you don't love them. Think clearly about what arrangement you'd like to try and suggest to them that you put it into action for a trial period.

3. **Set Limits on Contact.**

   If you feel like your parents are demanding too much contact:

   a. Start with a compliment: "I'm very happy that you love me so much that you want to talk to me often. I love you too."

   b. Fill them in on your dilemma: "I'm trying so hard to study and build a life at the university. By taking care of what I need to at school, I feel like I'm disappointing you because my time with you is limited. This distracts me from my work."

   c. Plan for the future: "I'm hoping that you can understand that and together we can establish a system that works well for all of us."

   d. If they give you a lot of flack, add: "The more you push me to contact you, the more you push me away. I don't think you mean to have this effect, but that's what happens."

4. **Introduce Your Parents to E-Mail.**

   The mismatch in schedules and in desire for frequency of contact could be resolved by supplementing the phone with E-mail. You grew up with computers and high technology, whereas your parents did not. Offer to help them set up a computer and give them an E-mail lesson. Holding their hand for a few hours could have a huge payoff down the road. Encourage them to get a computer and on-line service provider maintenance contracts that include technical support so that they won't be calling on you when things go awry.

5. **Make Visits Home as Enjoyable as Possible.**

   a. Suggest that you collaboratively devise guidelines for living together again. If they insist on laying down the law, you can remind them that you've handled your freedom well so far and have gotten used it. You hope that they'll trust you a little more. If the situation feels so restrictive that you feel less inclined to spend time at home, let them know that this might affect how long you visit next time, and that it would sadden you to cut the time short.

   b. If you feel torn between peers and parents, then consider finding ways to combine the two worlds during your visits. Dinners, movies, playing sports, and board games are often the more the merrier.

   c. Be aware that you might revert back to old, more childlike habits when you're around your parents. Maybe you just like being nurtured for a change, or perhaps you think they won't respond well to how mature you've become. Let them see how grown-up you are—relationship benefits just might flow.

d. If you're visiting home very often and are upset that your parents don't seem excited enough to see you, then stay away for longer increments and give them a chance to miss you.

6. Negotiating Contact When Your Parents Are Apart.

a. Keeping divorced parents up-to-date can be a snap with E-mail. You can write one message and use it several times by adding a personal greeting and sign-off. Of course, edit according to how personal you get with each parent, and make sure to use the phone as well.

b. If you have a preferred visiting schedule based on your workload and when your neighborhood friends are going to be around, then make your wishes known. If your parents fight over you, offer them motivation to resolve their differences. Let them know that they aren't considering the third option you might institute if they don't let up: your staying at school or visiting a school pal's family for a vacation. To make your time off from school pleasant, they have to put some effort into behaving themselves.

7. Opening Up to Parents.

a. Decide what you need to keep private in order to feel like your own person. Decide what you might enjoy sharing. Condition your parents so that they learn which types of questions will yield responses and which won't. Unless they resort to water torture to extract the information from you, they can't make you talk. It's this fact that may frustrate them most of all.

b. Instead of waiting for them to ask, offer up information that you're comfortable sharing. This will help reassure them that you do want to relate to them, even if you appropriately don't want to divulge all.

c. If they persist in asking you questions that you don't want to answer, try a straightforward response with a little humor, "That question won't get you very far. Why don't you ask me about X or let's go do Y."

d. If you tend to divulge all, don't feel embarrassed, it's great that you feel close to your parents. Do, however, ask yourself whether or not it would be good for you to open up more to other people in your life as well. A gradual shifting from your parents to your peers as your most intimate confidants would be a good long-term goal.

CHAPTER 7

Student Decision-Making
How to Help Your Child Problem-Solve

Your child is in your tender loving care and you want to protect her from harm. As a baby when she first learned to walk, you hoped she wouldn't stroll into sharp objects. When she started school, you prayed that she would make friends. When school became more academically demanding, you tried to have faith that she would succeed. When she started travelling places on her own, you prayed that she would be safe. When her peers started drinking and dating, you hoped that she would stay out of danger.

Over the years, your child became more and more independent. With each step of independence, you experienced new gratification, accompanied by new concerns. As your control over your child's environment diminished, your concerns grew greater. Now, your child is off to college. Although you no longer worry about her walking into harmful objects, all the other concerns still hold and are magnified by the fact that she's living out of the house. Not to mention all the new concerns that are added: Will she choose a promising career path? Will she handle finances responsibly? Will she and her roommate get along? Will she fall in love and run off with her lover?

Anita, a mom: What I find most difficult about having your children leave for college is the loss of control you feel as a parent. When they're little, you have them under your wing, so to speak. You can protect them and you can control a lot of their life to make it pretty good. It's not that I want control now, but the hardest part for me during this transition is seeing your kids taking control and not always doing the best thing. You want your kid to go to college, but you got all of your eggs in one basket—there is a whole lot of nurturing that went into that little creature.

It's not easy watching your child march off into the world. But it's not as if you're sending him out there without any defenses. Through your parenting over the years, you've armed your child with competencies and modeled ways to handle life's challenges. Plus, he may be leaving, but you're not going anywhere. You remain a solid foundation, waiting there to support him when he needs it. You are the secure base he can use to get him through the insecurities he'll face in the new universe of university. Think of yourself as an expert consultant on the topic of life.

What the Parental Imagination Can Conjure Up

Before we dive into the depths of worry and how to cope, let's have a little fun. Please fill in the blanks about your child's favorites:

Leisure activity:_____

Name of a cable TV station:_____

TV show:_____

Dessert food:_____

Fast food: _____

Vegetable: _____

Number between one and ten:_____

Color: _____

Animal in plural:_____

Sport:_____

Type of place:_____

Type of place:_____

Type of place:_____

Major bathroom fixture:_____

Body part: _____

Letter between G and Z: _____

A different letter between G and Z: _____

Luxury small plural objects: _____

Now take the items you chose and enter them into the following story:

My Son Loves College—A Little Too Much?

My child seems to have adapted quite happily to college life. He's free to (leisure activity) _____ rather than attend class. If he does make it to a class, then it's the perfect time for him to catch up on his sleep; he dreams of (the same leisure activity) _____. It's not that he's exhausted from studying all night, no. It's due to the fact that (name of a cable TV station) _____ plays reruns of (TV show) _____ until 4:00 A.M.

My son the college student isn't at all phased by the fact that the meal plan food isn't as tasty as his family's home-cooking; he's perfectly content eating (dessert food) _____ for breakfast, lunch, and dinner, along with (fast food) _____ for snacks. He better enjoy solid foods while he can; by the end of the school year he'll be stuck eating (vegetable) _____ baby food because he'll be lucky if he has (number between one and ten) _____ teeth left.

The fact that he can actually wash his own laundry seems to have brought him a certain degree of notoriety on campus. Everybody waves as they walk by, "Hey, (color) _____ guy"—the result of his washing colors with whites on the hot water setting. He may be clean, but he still manages to smell—on purpose! Proudly applying his biology coursework to everyday life, he's decided that if (animal in plural) _____ attract mates by emitting their natural odors, pheromones, then he would do the same; he stopped wearing deodorant.

His pheromone approach wasn't working too well for him until the (sport) _____ coach took him off the bench and put him among the first string of players. Now he attracts so many women that he has to make sure they don't all run into each other; so on his dates, he takes one to the (type of place) _____, and another to the (type of place) _____, and another to the (type of place) _____. He doesn't need to go to bars to meet women, the co-ed bathroom (major bathroom fixture) _____ will do. He's learned from upper-class males how to pick up female dormmates and their friends by asking for feminine expert advice on how to clean his (body part) _____.

He can keep track of every woman's phone number, every music CD, and every sports magazine, yet conveniently misplaced his glasses the day his grades were posted. He reported to us that he got two (letter between G and Z) _____s and three (letter between G and Z) _____s. Another thing he reports lost often is money—dollar bills falling through holes in his pockets since his mom isn't there to do his mending. Then how does he find enough money to fill his dorm room with (luxury small plural objects) _____?

All in all, I think my son is happy with his adjustment to college. The question is, "Am I?"

I'm sure that if I asked you to fantasize about the worst that your child could be up to, you'd be able to, if you haven't already. The trick is learning how to keep your concerns under control so that you can sleep easy by night and support your child by day.

Keeping Worries in Perspective
Change assister parents worry about how their college-aged kids are doing, but manage to keep their fears in perspective. Rather than dwell on their kids' weaknesses, they remind themselves of their children's strengths:

Sally, a mom: *With Heather, it seems like she is ready to be out in the world; so it's time to let her do that. I feel comfortable doing that because I feel comfortable with the decisions that she makes and the friends that she chooses. Also, I trust her to ask others or us for help or information if she needs it.*

Of course it helps when the child's maturity level warrants confidence. Even when change assister parents have real concerns based on their kids' past troubles in high school, they try to communicate confidence before they feel it. They give their child the benefit of the doubt while they wait and see how the child will adjust.

Many change assister parents have a calm attitude about life in general. They accept their own fallibility. They've made mistakes in their lives and recovered, so why won't their children? They consider mistakes to be human, inevitable, and good learning tools. They know that when a child learns from her mistakes, she grows stronger and is better able to tackle the world on her own. Typically, most kids of change assisters prove their parents correct by becoming more competent over time.

Some change assister parents fall on the worrier end of the scale, but take responsibility for keeping their worry under control. Sometimes their full, busy lives keep them sufficiently distracted. Other times, these parents have to actively prevent their worry from spilling over into their children's lives:

Martin, a father: *I have a psychological problem with doom and gloom—I'm always somehow fearful that she'll be riding in a car and be hurt, or that something else bad is going to happen. When I'm worried about my daughter, rather than put my worries on her, I jog with my business partner every morning and we always chat about different things. Just talking about it helps. Then, if the concern is still on my mind, I'll say to my wife, "Eva, I know I'm off the wall on this one, but I'm feeling like I want to do this—what do you think?"*

Asking people you trust for a reality check is a good way to go: "How worried should I really be?" Upon getting reassurance, it can be very stress-relieving to laugh at how your concern can get blown out of proportion. Of course it's key to consult people who are calmer by nature than you are. Otherwise, the consultation session can quickly turn into a worry fest. If the calm person agrees with your concerns, then you can problem-solve together.

With change resister parents, however, worry often gets the best of them:

Adam, a student: *Soon after I left for college, my mom started calling me up frequently because she had specific questions to ask like am I eating? Did I take care of this and that? She'll remind me, "Don't forget to bring your coat. Study hard. Wash up at night, and lock your door so you don't get your stuff stolen." I feel that my parents shouldn't be that concerned about my well-being because it's a pretty safe environment up here, and there are 30,000 other college students just like me.*

The most real danger isn't that your child will fail in life, but that your worry will convey that you lack faith in her abilities.

Demonstrating Confidence in Your Child

The best way to foster competence in children is to show them that you believe they can do it. When your child was learning how to walk, you said, "You can do it." When he was learning how to ride a bike, you said, "You can do it." Now that he's heading off to college, it's also time to say, "You can do it." You probably know this already, but it's one of those easier-said-than-done situations.

Think about life with your own parents when you were growing up; did they have confidence in your ability to succeed in life? How did their view of you influence how you saw yourself? In turn, how did your self-esteem affect your path in life?

Parents are by far the most powerful self-esteem reflectors in a person's life—whether the person is twelve years old or thirty. If you demonstrate confidence in your child, she will feel sure of herself. Feeling self-confident, your child is more likely to introduce herself to her classmates and win their friendship. She's more likely to take classes that interest and challenge her and to live up to that challenge. If she's confused about a point in class, she's more likely to approach the professor or a teaching assistant with her question. If she's faced with peer pressure to do drugs, she's more likely to say, "No thanks." If, however, your child sees fear and disappointment reflected back to her, then she's more likely to stumble and not pick herself up again. Your worry becomes a self-fulfilling prophecy.

What if your child has already given you major concerns, because she's flunking out of classes or out drinking every single night until 4:00 A.M.? The actions in this chapter will give you practical advice on how to assess the seriousness of the situation and come to your child's aid.

The reflection of herself that your child sees in your eyes is more meaningful to her than the reflection she sees from anybody else; your confidence carries a lot of weight.

Hoping for the best and worrying are two different things. The former shows your child that you care, the latter can convey mistrust. Mistrust strains relationships. Your child feels not only more distant from you, but also like she's a bad person because she's causing you, her beloved parent, anguish:

Samantha, a student: I hate the fact that my mom is always worrying about me. Because then I feel guilty and partially responsible for her distress.

Of course you don't necessarily mean to induce feelings of guilt in your child, but this is what happens. Perhaps your worry is fueled by your own guilt that you can't protect your child in the ways you would like.

Have you thought to yourself at any point during this transition process, "I'd worry so much less about my child if only she could stay home and I could continue watching out for her"? Believe it or not, parents of commuter students have many similar worries to parents of residential students, with the added fears that come with the act of commuting, especially by car. Seeing your child every day can even intensify a parent's fears:

Jennifer, a student: Mom constantly tells me about the stories in the paper, about how somebody was mugged and somebody was this and that. Every time something happens she says, "Be careful and always look around you." She warned me about not taking any late classes or walking to my car after dark. I can understand where she is coming from, but I'm a little annoyed.

As one student who lives at home said, "Between the actual commute and concerns about safety, commuting to school takes up as much energy as a class." So if having your child live at home isn't the answer, then what's a worrier to do? Plenty, read on.

ACTION
The More Relaxed You

1. **Pinpoint Your Concerns.**
   a. Make a list of your worries and next to each write down the vulnerabilities your child displays that add to your concern. Then assess whether or not your worries are based more on your child's weaknesses or your own tendency to fret. If your own worries win out, then find a calm person to whom you can talk about your concerns. If your child's weaknesses win out, then follow the advice in this chapter on how to support him appropriately.

b. Contemplate how your child coped with her weaknesses before; are these weaknesses that you've battled as well and how have you managed? Think about times you and your child have made mistakes and recovered.

2. **Get in Touch with the Confidence You Do Have in Your Child.**

a. Make a list of your confidences and next to each write down the strengths your child displays that you find reassuring. Recall times when you felt confident and proud of your child or when she surprised you with her display of maturity. Keep this list on hand as a reminder of how you can balance your concerns with your confidences. Give yourself credit for helping to foster these strengths in your child.

b. Let your child know that you believe in his capabilities and maturity. Be careful not to set up unreasonable expectations and not to be dismissive of his own concerns. Being tuned into who your child is, including his strengths and weaknesses, will make him feel loved, accepted, and understood. The key isn't to deny his vulnerabilities, but to show him that you're not panicking over them, and to let him know that you believe he can overcome them.

3. **If You're a Worrywart, There's Hope.**

a. Ask yourself, "Am I somebody who always needs something to worry about? If I can't find the obvious concern, do I then delve until a worry unearths itself?" If the answer is yes, then remind yourself that having a precious child away in a new environment is fertile ground for you to invent concerns that you don't need to have.

b. If you have dreams in which your child keeps getting into danger and trouble, then be reassured that you're not having premonitions, you're just anxious. Your unconscious is grappling with all your worries while you're trying to sleep.

c. Joke with your child that you know you're a worrywart. Send him a copy of the children's story of Chicken Little who runs around warning, "The sky is falling. The sky is falling." Add the caption, "Chicken Little, AKA Your Mother." Making a little fun of yourself magically turns your less attractive traits into charming quirks.

d. If somebody you know and trust lives near your child's campus, then arrange for all of you to have dinner together and hang out for an evening. These friends could become your child's home away from home. Of course you can't force the bond, but if it happens, great.

4. Express Concern as Empathy Not Inquiry.

Ask questions that show your concern for how your child is feeling, not ones that demand a report of how she is doing. In other words, rather than asking, "Are you eating? Going to classes? Studying?" try asking, "How's the food—edible? Do you like your professors? Are they dynamic or boring? What are your favorite classes? Have you found a good study spot you like? Is the workload reasonable?" These revised questions communicate that you don't expect it all to be easy going, plus you're lending an ear.

5. Make Good Use of Your Personal Experiences.

If your child is struggling with an issue and you've been there yourself, share your story. If you encountered emotional difficulties when you left home, communicate your experiences and how you managed. If you can admit to making mistakes, she can admit them too. Make sure to communicate how you think she and you are similar and different, and how this will play into how similar or dissimilar you predict her experience will be. Kids like to feel acknowledged as separate individuals.

6. Help Your Child Come to Her Own Conclusions.

a. Ask wise questions that gently guide your child toward a rational exploration of all the important angles of the dilemma. Your stock phrases might include "What are the pros and cons of . . ." or "I see that, but what if. . . ." Be careful not to go into the questioning with an agenda; your child will pick up on this immediately. In the exploration process, you just might discover something new as well. This technique will not only help your child come to a sound conclusion on the issue at hand, but will also increase her overall self-confidence and problem-solving ability.

b. When your child asks you directly for advice, reply, "Let's examine the issue together." After you collaboratively come up with pros and cons, and are ready for the conclusion, say, "So, what do *you* think you should do?" This method works well for all students, especially those who tend to depend on their parents too much.

7. Be a Good Role Model.

As a singer-songwriter friend of mine wrote, "Words whisper and actions shout." The most powerful tool you have at your disposal is to be a positive role model. Think of what behaviors and skills you'd like your child to develop. If you don't display them yourself, then acquire them.

8. Encourage Your Child to Take Advantage of the Various Student Support Services on Campus.

Most universities have a counseling center that handles all adjustment problems, whether they be academic, peer, or family related. For academic assistance, there are tutoring centers, graduate student teaching assistants (TAs), and professors' office hours. Some colleges have a buddy system in which either an upper-class member or an alumnus is assigned to a new student as a knowledgeable guardian angel, so to speak. The latest trend in student support involves life skills classes on relationships, money management, and study skills, which students can take through the university, sometimes even for credit. Research found that students who take the courses are more likely to stay in school and perform better academically.

Safety

What is the top concern on your mind for your child at school? The worry that tops most parents' list is physical safety. Parents think about their daughters and sons walking home late at night from a study session or heading out into the nearest urban center for some fun, and envision them being mugged or assaulted. The safety concern is heightened when their child's school is located in an environment that is more urban than the hometown:

Charlene, a student: The biggest concern on both my parents' minds was my being in a city environment. I've always lived in the suburbs—in a very sheltered suburb at that—where you can always walk the streets at one in the morning, walk home from a friend's house and you don't have any problems at all. You know everybody that lives on your block and that kind of thing.

Why does the safety concern consume parents most? First of all, it's the aspect of their child's being away from home that parents feel the least like they can have any control over. After all, you can offer to get your child academic tutoring, but you can't rent her bodyguards. Well you could, but she wouldn't have any friends left after being seen on campus being trailed by the Secret Service, and she probably wouldn't talk to you much anymore.

Second, you imagine that your child's physical safety isn't just out of your hands, but also out of hers. This is where you are wrong. Your child can do much to keep herself safe from harm, and you can be an important advisor in this area. Street smarts isn't a character trait somebody is born with; it's an acquired skill. The action tips (see pages 142–44) will inform you as to how your child can develop safety awareness.

Third, disquieting images of your child in danger are vivid because you probably consume the news in one form or another, whether it be through newspapers, TV, or magazines. Of course the press is going to highlight and sensationalize all the wrongdoing that goes on, especially when bad things happen to innocent kids. Acts of international terrorism get loads of media play, leading people to believe that travel is unsafe, yet the odds of being a victim of terrorism are infinitesimally low. In the same way, the media misleads you to believe that your college kid is in danger. If universities were deadly places, people would stop sending their kids to them and everybody would be a mail-order college graduate.

Even though universities can't treasure your child like you do, colleges do have an important investment in your child's safety—a college's image is everything to its financial survival. If the public were to view it as unsafe, then parents would not allow their kids to attend and it would go bankrupt. Universities provide many services designed to keep your children safe, from emergency call buttons in bathrooms, to security checks in dorm lobbies, to escort services on campus.

Change Assisters Versus Resisters
Most change assister parents keep their safety concerns in perspective and come to terms with the limitations of their parental reach:

Francesca, a mom: I am concerned. But it's not a neurotic concern. It's just that there are elements that I can't protect her from. Even if I lived there, I couldn't. You can't put a bubble around your child; you can't put them in a plastic cocoon and keep them safe forever. While I was concerned, I didn't let it get out of hand.

Change resisters understand that as kids grow up in the world and spend more time on their own, there's a certain amount of risk involved, but they fight this inevitability:

Adam, a student: My mom goes, "Well, why do you want to live so far away? It's dangerous." She says to me, "Stay away from the hoodlums around school. Try not to go home too late because there are a lot of bad people out there—you've got to be careful." I thought, "Don't you trust me that I know how to take care of myself? You don't have to baby me around all these years; I can go out once in a while."

Excessive fear on your part could easily make your child feel like the world is a horribly dangerous place and lead her to doubt her own ability to protect herself. What matters most when it comes to warding off an attack isn't the specific self-defense tactic employed, e.g., walking under street lights, but the fact that the person believes in the form of self-protection she's using. As a parent, you want to make sure that you foster and don't undermine whatever air of self-assurance your child projects.

Rather than asking your child frequently if she's walking alone at night and locking her door, try offering your child a few safety tips or subsidize a self-defense class. Then, every now and then ask your child, "Is there anything you need to help you feel more safe and secure over there or are you fine?" In this way, you're not checking up on her, yet you're letting her know that you're there to help out if she needs you. Then, if you express your concern over a truly serious situation, such as a hurricane in the area, your child will more likely be responsive. However, if you're fretting over her all the time, she won't take you seriously when you really really mean it; the old story about the boy who cried wolf comes to mind.

Drawing Comfort from the Past
One way that change assister parents comfort themselves is by thinking about the times when their child functioned well out there in the big bad world:

David, a dad: I am very comfortable with her being out in the world. She had been to a number of places that I had never been to, and I have been to a number of places in the world. I was not concerned about her; I felt that she was fairly streetwise.

If you're a change resister parent, there may be nothing your child can do to prove to you that she knows how to handle herself well enough to avoid danger. One young woman kept herself perfectly safe while traveling through Europe completely alone, and still her father worried terribly about her at school. She could walk through a war zone untouched and he would still probably always imagine the worst.

Are you the type of person who always wants loved ones to call when they've reached their destination? Do you take down detailed flight information when your children and spouse fly and then call the airlines to make sure that the plane arrived safely? Do you identify with the mother being described by her husband: "Even if it were a sterile environment inside a big bubble with security guards for every person, my wife would still be concerned"? If you answered yes to any of these questions, then you are a worrywart. Perhaps you were raised by cautious parents, or were unfortunate and experienced the illness or death of somebody you held close to your heart. Whatever the reason, having your child living at school will make you anxious, but you can cope. Following these tips will help.

ACTION
Easing Your Mind

1. Take Media News with a Grain of Salt.

Reading about robberies, shootings, and rapes every day can increase your worry quotient. If a particular bit of news is troubling you, then find out whether or not your spouse and friends think the event will have an impact on your child.

2. Think About All the Times Your Child Has Proven Her Ability to Take Care of Herself.

Recall times when she traveled overnight, made day pilgrimages to a big city, or went overseas. How did she handle herself? Did she return in one piece? My guess is that she did. Think of the number of days your child has been alive and the number of days within that that she's been safe. Hopefully there's a one-to-one correlation between the two.

3. Research What Safety Measures the University Takes.

Parent orientation programs address this topic, and a call to the dean of students' office should bring you information as well. The university gives your child safety information during the student orientation program; but if you're wondering whether or not your child knows of the services, why not ask casually? As long as you're not investigating whether or not she uses them, it can't hurt to inform her about what's available.

4. Offer Safety Tips.

a. Let your child know that you trust her; it's the new environment that you mistrust. Ask her what precautions she's developed on her own over the years, and use these as building blocks.

b. Tell your child about special precautions you take when walking alone at night and safety measures that have failed you. Imparting stories along with the advice will help the information stick in her mind.

c. Offer standard tips, such as walking under the street lamps, looking like you know where you're going, and putting pride aside so that you can back away from verbal confrontations. Here are a few more:

- Develop your peripheral vision so that you can see well on either side of you even when looking straight ahead. Look behind you every now and then. If somebody suspicious-looking is lurking around, look at this person; let him know that you know he is there. Duck into the nearest store.

- If you have something in your backpack that's of great personal value, such as a computer disk with your term paper on it, carry it in your pocket; this way, if a thief demands your bag, you can give it up without the slightest hesitation. Also make sure that your bag doesn't hold your keys and address. It's helpful to carry your keys in your hand anyway so that you're ready to enter your apartment or car quickly.

For more safety tips, go to the New York University website at www.nyu.edu and search for "safety"; any guidance that is useful for the Big Apple will certainly help anywhere in the country. Remember, it's not exactly what your child does or doesn't do that matters, it's the fact that she believes in the effectiveness of her own techniques that counts.

d. Avoid using this as an opportunity to try to steer your child away from certain behaviors you disapprove of. For instance, if it makes you uncomfortable that your daughter dresses in miniskirts, don't say, "Dress less sexily." Instead, suggest she wear a long coat on the way to the party.

e. Recommend a self-defense class. Schools generally offer self-defense or martial arts classes. If he takes a class the summer before college begins, you could even join him in a course that includes parents. A class should be only of his choosing.

f. Let her know that you're always there in case of an emergency, that you will do whatever is in your power to help, that you won't judge her, and that you will try hard not to panic.

5. Discuss Ways Your Child Can Protect His Property.

Advise your child to not leave his bag, books, and class notes lying around in the library if he takes a study break or goes to the bathroom. Locking his dorm door when he's not there or when he's sleeping isn't a bad idea either. Of course that's the type of decision that has to be made with a roommate, and requires taking the dorm atmosphere into account. If everybody else on your child's floor has an open-door policy, and he doesn't, then he could pay a social cost by locking up. Your child might want to consider leaving anything valuable and irreplaceable at home.

6. Familiarize Yourself with the Campus and Surrounding Area.

a. Buy a guidebook for the city and read up on what the area has to offer and if there are any parts of town that are considered less desirable. There's nothing better than taking a trip to the area if you can afford it. Check out the campus and surrounding neighborhood at different times of day. The better you get to know the area and observe other students walking around safely, the more you'll be able to relax.

b. If you can't visit, then inquire whether the university has produced a video or website that could give you a visual introduction to the area. Don't rely on movies that take place in the city; remember, movie plots strive to create drama—drama is what you don't need.

7. Cell Phones Can Be Useful as Emergency Backups.

What college student would refuse the gift of a cell phone? Only if there are strings attached—strings that reach all the way back to her parents. Make it clear that you don't expect her to use it to check in with you. If you can't afford to have her talking on it all the time, then let her know it's for emergencies. Be forewarned: The temptation to use the phone for chitchat may be too great for any student to resist. Although there are cell phones that just dial 911, your child will be less likely to carry this around with her.

Health and Self-Maintenance

Do you imagine your child eating pizza for breakfast, lunch, and dinner? Picture him falling asleep in class and walking around campus in his bathing suit because he ran out of clean clothes? You're not the only one and, on some days, this vision might not be too far from the truth. The good news is that no college student ever died from an overdose of cola and pizza, lack of sleep, or grubby socks. Don't worry, your child won't lose friends due to dirty laundry because most students are on the same laundry schedule—wash when you're down to your last pair of undies. Sloppiness is another low alienation risk trait; notice how dorm rooms don't appear in *House and Garden*.

Self-Maintenance Concerns Are Overrated

For laundry give a few tips, tell him you're available for advice, and be glad that he's the one giving his clothes the sniff test. For sleep, he's just going to have to find the right balance between work, play, and rest. With a roommate's comings and goings to contend with, recommend earplugs.

Is your child on the meal plan? Are you concerned that she may just nibble on the main courses, gobble down the dessert, and then head out for a hamburger joint at midnight? The freedom of not having somebody telling you what to eat, combined with ever-present fast, cheap junk food is too tempting for many students to pass up. Yet, be reassured: This pattern usually doesn't last more than a semester or two. Eventually, students realize that poor eating habits are zapping their energy, which they need in order to stay on top of their studies and social lives. If worse comes to worst, remind yourself that there are plenty of Americans who subsist only on greasy fast food.

Remind yourself that the tomato sauce on pizza counts as a vegetable according to the USDA Food Guide pyramid, and according to research, fights cancer. Although I provide a few tips for helping her eat well, there is a fair amount of tongue-biting in store for you when it comes to her health habits. Feed your child well when she comes home for vacations, and she'll begin to see the difference nutrition can make.

While odds are that your child doesn't have an eating disorder, the transition to college is a high-risk time for developing one, second only to puberty. With American society putting pressure on females to match the stick-thin body beautiful ideal, it's no wonder that females with anorexia (slow starvation) or bulimia (bingeing and purging) outnumber males nine to one. Be on alert, however, that eating disorders among males are on the rise.

Family issues of control can play a large role in the development of eating disorders during this period of readjustment. When parents try to keep their kids at home and dependent during college, struggles over who controls the child's life can spark eating disorders. The child needs some way to assert independence, and denying herself food may seem like the only route.

Have you imagined dorms as breeding grounds for germs? While students aren't going to contract life-threatening, debilitating diseases, they will likely catch a cold or flu that's going around, just as they did when they started kindergarten. At worst, they'll suffer through a bout of mononucleosis. While flu shots are far from 100 percent guaranteed protection, they're not a bad idea.

When your child was living under your roof there wasn't that much you could actually do to prevent seasonal illnesses, but you did provide tender loving care for a speedy recovery. How can you care for a sick child over the telephone? This section's tips provide a few ideas.

Be a Health Role Model

A "Do as I say, not as I do" stance is never as effective as a "This works well for me, it will likely work for you" approach. Do you take good care of yourself? Or do you smoke, drink, eat poorly, sleep rarely, overwork yourself, or not go to the doctor nor take your medication when you need to? Your kid takes notice if you don't do what you can to keep yourself healthy:

Lori, a student: My senior year of high school, Dad had a heart attack because of his cholesterol problem. And he's so stubborn that he won't admit that he has the cholesterol problem. The doctor's been telling him, "If you don't start eating right and laying off all this stress, you know you could die." He says he is eating right, but I don't believe him, because he's so stubborn he just doesn't want to admit he has this problem. Also, he doesn't stick to his exercise program, so I have to tell him to exercise.

Paul, a student: My dad had an angina attack and was admitted to the hospital. My mom thinks he's having chest pains again but he won't admit it until pretty much he's passed out on the floor. My mom told me that I should make him get a physical. I plan to tell him that if he doesn't do it for himself, he should do it for his son, Paul. I'm majoring in biology and I've worked as an Emergency Medical Technician. I feel that since I have all this knowledge about the body, I should be taking care of him and if anything does happen—if I didn't act fast enough—then maybe it was my fault.

Not only are these kids denied a healthy parental example, but also they are stuck in a secure base reversal; they feel personally responsible for trying to get their parents to take better care of themselves. With so much worry and stress, their own self-care and health are likely to suffer. Feeling like their parents' lives could quite literally be in their hands is no small burden. You can say to your child that he's not responsible for your health over and over again until you're blue in the face, but it won't make any difference. If there's even the slightest chance that what he says to you will make the difference between life and death, then he's going to keep trying to figure out how he can word his statements just right to persuade you to change.

By taking good care of yourself, you have everything to gain. Don't you want to live long enough to see your child graduate from college, embark on a career, settle down, and start a family of his own? If you have any doubt, then think about the possibility of your child following in your unhealthy footsteps; wouldn't you rather be a positive role model that helps *him* live longer? Unhealthy habits can be hard to break. By definition, a habit is learned, so there is no reason that it can't be unlearned as well.

ACTION
Parental Tender Loving Care

1. **Upping Your Child's Nutritional Intake.**
   a. Give your child a bottle of once-a-day multi-vitamins, along with a note

saying, "I thought this might help you keep your energy up for your fast-paced lifestyle."

b. Offer a few cooking lessons that emphasize fast and healthy meals or ones that will impress the socks off of everybody on the dorm floor.

c. Send a care package full of healthy foods and snacks, like raisins and nuts, but also make sure to include some borderline foods, such as hot cocoa mix and granola bars; you don't want your child to think that you're trying to mother him from miles away, even though you are. Sign your child up for the fruit of the month club (e.g., the Harry and David company at 1-800-345-5655), and maybe a cheese club for variety. These companies will send a box of food to your child's doorstep every month; with twenty mangoes, there will be more than enough for him to share, making him popular and healthy all at once. If you go on a trip to Florida, send your child a box of oranges.

d. Read up on nutrition yourself; *The American Dietetic Association's Complete Food and Nutrition Guide* by Roberta Larson Duyff (New York: John Wiley & Sons, 1998) is a thorough and fun resource. You might pick up some tips along the way, improve your health, and become an excellent role model. You could say to your child, "I just learned that adding peanut butter to my toast with jam in the morning can keep me more awake and alert. I highly recommend it."

2. **How to Detect If Your Child Has an Eating Disorder.**

a. Snacking too much while studying or not eating much for a week because she's nervous about exams do not constitute an eating disorder. Here are a few signs to look out for that can be detected during a visit of a few days: wanting to eat in private; hardly eating anything at all; bizarre food rituals, such as cutting up what's on her plate into zillions of tiny pieces; disappearing into the bathroom after every meal; always measuring and criticizing her own weight; exercising rigorously and frequently, not for athletic training, but for fear of gaining weight; and the gaunt appearance of an anorexic or the swelled-up look of a bulimic with puffy "chipmunk" cheeks.

b. If you suspect that your daughter has an eating disorder:

• Let her know that the changes you see in her mood and behavior concern you; you miss the old her.

- You can ask her if there are any troubles she's had lately for which she'd like a sympathetic ear. Ask her how she's been feeling about her body. Be aware that most people with eating disorders are in denial about their struggles; they often think that other people are simply jealous of their display of slenderness and great restraint. She may get angry in response to your concern. Ride the tide of hostility.
- Ask her if she'll humor you by visiting her old doctor to put your parental fears to rest. Obviously, you can't force her to go.
- If your concern is growing, gather together family and friends who have also noticed the drastic changes and hold an intervention; with the help of a professional counselor, you express your love and concern for your daughter, along with a confrontation about her self-destructive behavior.

3. What You Can Do If Your Child Is Under the Weather.

a. Offer generous doses of empathy, along with calm, soothing, loving messages. Remind him of what helped ease his symptoms when he was living at home. It never hurts to give your "Here's what to do to get better" speech. Send him his favorite novel or the latest CD by his favorite band.

b. If symptoms persist or seem odd, encourage him to call the campus health advice line and see a doctor. Try to avoid being the hypochondriac, panicked parent. Instead start out as the empathic one, "You must be tired of being sick. Go get some medical attention and I'll cover the bill."

c. Giving your child health insurance is the best gift of all. Trust me, if your child has to ask you for money for each doctor's bill or foot the bill himself, he's really not going to go.

4. Show Your Kid How It's Done.

a. Eat well. Make your diet balanced, and low in fat, sodium, and cholesterol.

b. Engaging in a physical activity three to four days a week for at least thirty minutes each time can reduce your risk of many different life-threatening diseases, from heart disease to cancer.

c. Quit smoking. Cigarettes are the leading cause of preventable deaths in the U.S. Quitting may be one of the hardest things you ever do, but you owe it to yourself and your child to do it. There are plenty of products and support groups to help you out.

d. Watch how much alcohol you drink. Sure, recent research shows that one glass of red wine a day can lower a specific type of cholesterol, but it also shows that drinking too much can cause major liver damage and kill you, not to mention the emotional and psychological toll it takes on you and your family. Congratulate yourself for admitting that you need help and then seek out counseling and support from groups like Alcoholics Anonymous (AA).

e. Visit the doctor on a regular basis, and if you're a woman, visit the gynecologist as well. Make sure that you have adequate health insurance.

f. Whatever bad habits you can't break, shield your child from observing them.

Academics

Remember when the college acceptance letter arrived for your child—how proud you felt. Recall at high school graduation when your child went on stage to receive her diploma—how proud you felt. Now that she's in college you're still beaming with pride, but your brow may also be furrowing from fret—what will her grades be?

You hope your child is studying as much as she needs to, and is not too distracted by partying. You hope she's excited about learning, and not feeling over her head in course work. Some kids are more studious than others. If your kid is a hard-core workaholic, then you may be more worried about whether she'll stick her head up long enough from the books to make friends. On the other hand, if your child becomes sidetracked easily, then it may be her studying fortitude that concerns you. Some high schools prepare kids for college better than others. College can be a challenge to even the most prepared high school student:

Greg, a dad: *When the high school student goes to college, there's often an initial shock—the realization that there will always be a lot of people who will be smarter than you. If you're doing well in high school, and then suddenly you're not doing as well as you'd like to be in college, then you begin to doubt yourself. Doubt is detrimental to a young student's development. You just have to give it the best you've got.*

Most college courses are graded on a curve, which means that there is a majority of parents out there whose college student children don't get

As, but who earn Bs, Cs, Ds, and even Fs. A student's performance may vary greatly depending upon the subject of the class.

Again, as a parent you have a delicate balance to find. You don't want to expect much more than your child can give because then he'll feel inadequate and insecure, because he knows he'll never be able to please you. On the other hand, you don't want to expect less than he can give because then he'll think that he won't be able to amount to much. A crystal ball would be nice, but you have a natural tool that's almost as good—your instincts.

Right now, ask yourself honestly, what you think your child's capabilities are in the various academic realms. What does your gut tell you? If he is doing the best he can, then it's your job as a parent to accept and love him for who he is. Let him know how proud you are of the efforts he's making and what he is achieving—he is in college after all. Congratulate any signs of progress. Help him discover his strengths that lie outside of academia. Maybe your child is more of a hands-on type of person who learns better on the job than in the classroom. Don't lose sight of the whole picture of who your child is; he may have many strengths that go unappreciated in an academic setting.

If, however, you think that he's not living up to his potential, then try to determine why not. Here's a checklist of the many possible reasons; check off the ones you think might apply.

_____ Taking on too much because he's so excited about learning.

_____ Not as well prepared from high school as many of the other students.

_____ Undisciplined when it comes to studying.

_____ Scared to try hard and find that he can't match the other students.

_____ Having trouble adjusting socially.

_____ Feeling depressed and therefore having difficulty concentrating.

_____ Stressing under pressure to please you; your standards for yourself and your child are particularly high.

_____ Distracted by the active social life and other activities.

_____ In trouble with alcohol or drugs.

_____ Unmotivated because he doesn't find his classes stimulating enough.

Did any of these possibilities ring true? You'll find sections in this chapter that address all of these scenarios in one form or another. Just getting a handle on the cause should help you relax somewhat and plan your next steps. If your son is dissatisfied with his own performance, then there's room for you to offer some guidance. If, however, you're the only one who's upset, then the checklist should help you to understand why you appear to be more worried about the matter than he is. In fact, it may be his lack of concern that concerns you as much as his non-stellar performance. You might be thinking, "If only he would start showing some desire to improve his grades, I could ease up." In all likelihood, the more you back off, the more he'll be able to admit to himself, and to you, that he too wants to improve.

Academic Adjustment

Keep in mind that it can take a few months, even a semester or two, for college students to adjust to the new academic demands. Here's what you might imagine: your child thinking, "I don't have anyone telling me what time to go to bed, I can stay up all night watching TV and partying. And then if I can't get out of bed to go to class, I don't have to. Pretty cool." Well, not only would this routine get old fast, but also the reality would hit: "Oops, I guess I can't get good grades and goof off all the time." Then he'd probably get his act together. Kids want to do well at least as much as you want them to, if not more, even if they don't fess up to this fact:

Elizabeth, a mother: I've wasted so much energy worrying when I really should have had so much confidence in my son, and confidence in the fact that, as parents, we're modeling an example that's really going to take. Every once in a while, I think, "My gosh, he wants to succeed more than I want him to succeed."

Even though they may not show it, most college students want to succeed in college even more than their parents want them to.

While students could sleep right through class, the vast majority don't. College classes, especially during freshman year, are so full that there's standing-room-only sections. Students want to make sure that they take good notes and learn firsthand what the homework assignments are.

When it comes to the balance between work and play, it may take your child a little time to figure out what he can "get away with." How late can he stay out and still be fresh for class? How much drinking will lead to a brain-clouding hangover? He will learn his lessons over time. Do you know any successful adults who were party animals in college? I bet you do; ask around. Besides, college students are generally aware that college is costing parents a lot of money and that there are limits to how much they should mess up.

College students are also figuring out exactly how much work they have to do to achieve certain results, the "when" of how much lead-time is needed for studying for an exam or writing a paper, and the "hows" of where to study and with whom. If your child is feeling blasé about courses in general, she should continue exploring different subjects; all it takes is one inspiring professor, one fascinating class, to spark her intellectual curiosity and set her study gears in motion.

While as a parent you might fear that poor grades earned during the adjustment period will ruin your child's chance of a prosperous future, the college isn't. Many employers and graduate admissions committees know that college students need to find their academic groove, so they often calculate a separate G.P.A. that excludes the freshman-year grades.

If you're genuinely concerned about how your child is adjusting academically, here are some actions you can take.

ACTION
Helping Your Child Flourish

1. **Bestow a Calm, Yet Realistic Confidence.**
   a. Rather than focusing on the specific letter grades your child is getting, tell him you know that it can take time to settle into a rhythm; you believe that he'll be able to do it. Panicking will only make him panic, too; panic isn't conducive to productive studying.
   b. Reassure him that it's a sign of strength to ask for assistance when you need it. If there was a time in your life when you asked for help, tell him that story; it will be easier for him to admit weakness when someone he looks up to has done it.

2. Problem-Solving with Your Child.

a. Pinpoint the sources of the difficulty, such as study environment, conflict with a professor/teaching assistant, or touching on an intellectual sore spot.

b. Attack each source, laying out a multi-pronged plan of action. She could consider tutoring services, seeking extra help from the TA or another student in the class, or changing the grade for the course to pass/fail to take the pressure off. If she's doing poorly and hates the material in the class, she could think about dropping it altogether. The grade change and drop options need to be done in a timely fashion; at a certain point in the semester they're no longer available. If it's the studying process that's the snag, then there's varying the study location and experimenting with earplugs, listening to mellow music on headphones, or turning the phone ringer off. If her class notes are a mess, then she could tape-record the lectures or take a laptop to class. Most universities offer workshops on study skills. She could find tips online (see Appendix). Consider the possibility that your child has a learning disability that wasn't detected in high school. Colleges often have services that can test for learning differences and difficulties.

3. Consider a Location Change.

a. Look into a study abroad opportunity. Most universities these days have programs in which students can earn credits while taking classes in a foreign country. Many students find this to be the highlight of their college career. It may be just what your child needs to jump-start her intellectual interest.

b. A college transfer may be in order. Educational philosophy, course offerings, and the student body vary from college to college. What your child may be experiencing is simply a mismatch between her and the school. Together, or with the help of a professional college advisor, figure out if there are better-suited schools. If she's uncertain, she can always apply for the transfer and visit campuses without committing. Just knowing that she has an escape hatch could take enough pressure off to help her settle into her current college.

4. Hold onto Your Seat Before You Read This One.

If your child is completely unhappy with college life in general, then perhaps taking a semester or more off might be the best approach. This is the type of option that's best if the idea comes from her. Some students require a little time out in the world before being able to appreciate and focus on college studies. These students often excel when they return, and even become their teachers' favorites.

Career Goals

If there's any area of a child's college career that parents have the most opinions about, it's got to be the choice of major. Close your eyes and picture your child where you hope she'll be in life ten years from now. Now imagine where your child will be ten years from now if she follows her heart, her dreams. Do these two images match? If yes, then that's terrific and certainly makes your life easier. Be forewarned that students often change their major in their college careers:

Greg, a change assister parent: I try to make him understand that there is an adjustment period and that he should explore until he finds out what he wants to do and where his aptitude is inclined. Some people explore for a few years, but some people even after four years don't know what to do. Some people change course in the middle of their careers after age forty. Only in very fortunate, gifted people is this not a problem. Like Mozart—no one had to tell him to write a symphony; he would just write it. Most of the children, I believe, will have to go through the discovery process.

College is most useful when it's used as a time of exploration, with the hope that by the end of the stint, the student will have found a career path that could lead her happily through life. More often than not, a satisfying career path is stumbled upon, inspired by a special professor or internship. The more your child feels free to explore, the greater the odds that she'll leave college headed in a satisfying direction. This section will help you aid your child in the discovery process.

The best use your child can make of a college education is to explore many different subject areas in her search for a satisfying professional life.

Parents' Professional Philosophies

Different parents have different philosophies about what the most important elements are of a good career; there's being your own boss, or having a higher education degree, or serving the community, or earning high
wages. Why so many different views? Because each parent is coming from
a different place in life:

Chandler, a dad: *I want to pass on to both of the children a pledge made*
by my father to his father. It goes like this: Service to humanity is the rent you
pay for occupying the space you have on this earth; so, would you please, Mr.
Next Generation, give something back to the world, to the community?

Neal, a student: *My dad tells me, "You should be a doctor or lawyer." He's*
a janitor and he came here when he was pretty young from San Salvador. So
he keeps telling me that he doesn't want me to have to pick up the broom and
clean up everyone else's mess.

It's great that parents hold different theories; diversity is what makes
the world go around; for civilization to persist, humanity needs people to
fulfill all the various functions in society. If everybody had the same career goals, competing for the same positions, refusing to do anything else
but that choice, then our culture would collapse.

There are, however, three important things to keep in mind. The first
is that your child be personally committed to the career path he chooses.
The second is that you communicate your views in such a way that your
child feels free to make his own choice: that he isn't worrying about disappointing you or losing your respect. And third is that you demonstrate
confidence in his ability to make healthy choices for himself.

The Bottom Line

Change assister parents may have strong feelings one way or another re-
garding the college major, but they know that the bottom line is that their
child must be happy with what he chooses:

Thomas, a dad: *Pamela should decide what she wants to do because she's going*
to live it. If I impose my preferences, then my daughter won't be comfortable,

and she won't be able to handle it all. It's up to her to decide what's good for her and what she thinks she can tackle. We'd rather have her make the mistake than try to get in and correct it. It's still her life, and she needs to make it what she wants it to be. If she wants the help, we'll be glad to give it to her.

Life will throw challenges your child's way. The greater her personal commitment to her job, the better will be her ability to overcome hurdles. If she loves her job, she might even be able to turn a challenge into an advantage, in the same way that a company which finds out that the competition is planning to come out with a similar product then develops a more innovative line.

If you're a change resister in this area, then you may find that your hopes and fears for your child's future overshadow what your child wants:

Adam, a student: *My mom wants me to be a doctor, and I'm interested in other things: political science, sociology, biology, and psychology. But, she's pushing doctor. I think she should leave the decision to me; stop putting pressure on me. It's going to be fifty years of my life of things that I hate. I feel like that's what my father's done. I don't want to repeat that.*

What philosophy did you live by when making your own choices? How did it turn out? Did you feel free to follow your heart? If not, why? How do you feel about the path you've taken?

It's important to remind yourself that your experiences and fears are not necessarily the same as those of your child. Circumstances have changed since you were growing up, both in your family and in the world. At the same time, remind yourself that you're smart. You've lived life with your eyes open and seeing quite a few things. Just as you shouldn't deny the worth of your child's views, you shouldn't deny the value of your own either. Your child looks up to you and regards your opinion as wisdom, even if she doesn't show it; use your influence wisely.

Communicating Your Views

Kids can feel completely overwhelmed by the demands of choosing a college major; the idea of deciding what you want to do in life is daunting at any age. So your child doesn't want you to seal your lips, but does want you to try to be as objective and supportive as you possibly can:

Max, a student: *If I propose a career goal to my dad, and he feels that I'm serious about something, he'll urge me towards it. If he feels that it's a whim, then he'll give me advice or just be interested. He'll step back and put himself in my shoes and say, "Gee, that's great, but what are you going to do about it? Have you thought about doing something in the summer or taking a course?" He gives me advice and encouragement in whatever I decide to do. Anytime I have a new idea, he says, "Good, go for it."*

Tone can mean everything when it comes to a conversation about career goals. Even if on the surface it appears as if you're dispassionately helping your child assess the good and the bad equally, if you have a clear agenda she picks up on it, because your kid is no dope:

Jasmine, a student: *My dad went through a list of possible careers and the pros and cons—job status, salaries, happiness, and the amount of work that goes into the job. I got this underlying sense that it would disappoint him if I get a job that he doesn't approve of. No matter what my parents say, "It's okay— whatever you choose, it's good for you," I still think it's a really big deal to them. And that's not a good thing for me. I have to ask myself, where do I draw the line between what I want and what my parents want? My dad didn't really urge me to pursue certain goals, but it was like a subtle shaping towards what he perceives as the best thing. That's really a confusing thing for me right now.*

The Negative Consequences of Battle over College Major It's difficult enough for college students to figure out which lines to draw within themselves in terms of their dueling desires, talents, and weaknesses. Add to the confusion pressure from parents to go in a certain direction and you've got a recipe for disaster: Trouble in the form of endless indecision, or ending up in major debt from an unwanted graduate school education, or following an unsatisfying path and feeling trapped. Another likely outcome is that your child will rebel by choosing a profession simply because you are vehemently against it. Then she winds up in a job that makes everybody unhappy, including herself:

Jordan, a Student: My mom was very happy when she first thought I would be going pre-med, and so she was very pushy about it. I told her last year that I took one art course, and that art was for me; she blew her stack. She was very, very upset, and she just pushed against it, again and again. She would say, "Do you really want to do that? How are you going to raise a family? You're going to be poor." Then I end up swinging from pre-med to art just as a reaction against what she wants.

When a child takes the path opposite her parents' wishes, it could also be curiosity that's fueling the move in the opposite direction. The more you say a profession is off-limits, the more intriguing that field becomes. A career choice with rebellion at its core may be even worse than one based on acquiescence because it has the added elements of guilt and self-doubt.

If your child pursues a career path that she's not personally committed to, then years of unhappiness may be ahead for her.

A person who lacks personal commitment to her career often winds up in crisis in her mid-thirties. You know what it means to work hard—to spend anywhere from eight to fourteen hours a day toiling at a job. Add up that number of hours over a lifetime and you'll find that the amount of time spent working is so huge it's beyond fathoming. Sad to say that the average American adult spends more hours at work than at any other activity, whether it be hanging out with family, engaging in a hobby, or sleeping. Feeling disconnected from a career can lead to serious relationship troubles down the road—not being able to commit to somebody, or feeling unworthy of love. Discontentment in a job often equals discontentment in life.

Sometimes the battle over career choice becomes so fierce that it prevents the parent-child pair from sharing any positive affection:

Paul, a student: When we're together we fight a lot, because we have different ideas about career. I want to make my own decisions. But he keeps pushing

*me in the direction he wants me to go. So when I'm here at school and we
don't talk as much, we get along a lot better.*

A typical resolution to battles over career goals is a "compromise" on
a double major:

James, a dad: *I do feel that my daughter should do something more practical
than psychology—something technical so that she can make money. She tells
people that she studies psychology for herself and statistics for me, to strike a
balance. She takes care of herself and doesn't disappoint me.*

While this may sound like a reasonable solution, it's not. A double major equals major stress. Students often have to struggle to meet the requirements for one major within four years, especially since there's
competition for classes that fill up fast. This path could compromise how
well she does in both areas and/or lead to an extended stay in school; and
you know what that means—extended costs!

Helpful Ways to Further Your Cause Believe it or not, leaving your child
to her own devices increases the chances that she might genuinely come
around to see the situation your way. With little investment in proving
your opinions wrong, she's free to explore. You're all on the same side—
waiting for the outcome of the experiment—instead of in opposition to
each other. If she comes to your very same conclusion on her own, then
this decision will have more staying power, and she won't have to wonder throughout her life, "What if . . . ?"

You may be thinking, "But if my child does in fact become a poet, a
rock 'n' roller, or a tennis player, then what? I don't want her to starve!"
A change assister answers your question:

Stanley, a dad: *I leave the decision up to my son. If he thinks that what he
really wants is to be an artist, then I say, "Being an artist is a difficult way to
get along and have enough food and shelter. How about being a bartender and
an artist, so that you can at least get enough money to live? Or how about
marrying a very rich woman?" So I try to move his imagination into multiple*

*possibilities. I urge him very strongly that if he gives up—if he disconnects
himself from his artistic loves—he will wither and die.*

It's realistic to think that artists find ways to supplement the income
from their art. In this day and age, temporary employment agencies are
placing people in jobs all the time, not to mention the way technological advances enable people to work from their homes. In this way, a
painter can run a graphic arts business on the side that supports her art.

Clearly if you care one way or another about your child's choices, you
won't be able to hide this fact. Nancy joked about her mom, "My mom
will say in the same sentence that she doesn't care about my career goals,
and then tell me exactly what she thinks I should do. I find this amus-
ing." You don't always have to be the perfect, neutral sounding board, but
at the very least, be up-front and soften your delivery. Say, "You know me,
I can't keep my opinions to myself. I don't expect you to follow my advice. I'll love and respect you the same whatever you do." This will cause
your child less internal conflict. Plus, you won't have pain from having to
bite your tongue.

Demonstrating Confidence Your child needs to know that you have confidence in his ability to make good decisions and succeed in his career of
choice. When giving advice, ground your comments in what you see as the
positive aspects of your child:

*Francesca, a mother: My daughter's considering going into law. I told her, "I
love the law. You're a person who feels the right and wrong of things, and
you're loyal to your friends and willing to fight for their causes. Maybe law is
a good way for you to go."*

Avoid statements that imply lack of faith in your child's ability to overcome occupational hazards or stereotypes:

*Sarah, a student: Since I was about ten, I always wanted to have a career
in politics or law. My mom is always saying to me, "Why would you want to
be a lawyer? Lawyers are slimy."*

While some lawyers are slimy, many are honest. What would lead a parent to believe that her child would take the low road? If there is any form of implied criticism in what you say, your child will find it. Unless you believe that your child can counter a specific professional stereotype, refrain from even mentioning it.

When advising your child on career goals, ground your comments in his strengths.

Despite the giant strides that women have taken in the work force over the past few decades, many parents today express doubt in their daughters' ability to balance work and family:

Mona, a mom: Samantha wants to study medicine, but also wants to have family and to have children. We said that she has to understand that the choices she makes have consequences for her life. If she wants to study medicine, she will be studying until she is twenty-seven, twenty-eight. If she wants to have children it will be later in her life. I want her to understand that I don't think that she could do both at the same time.

Granted, our society still has a long way to go when it comes to supporting working moms, but millions of women are leading a double life quite successfully. While life for supermoms is quite hectic, it's also incredibly rewarding. Show your daughter that you believe she can do it.

While your child picks up on any doubt you might communicate, your expressions of confidence can have a very positive effect:

Jimmy, a student: My dad has always been a source of confidence because he tries to convince my sister and me that we can do whatever we want to try to do. It leads you to believe you can; so you do do better.

You may feel powerless, but trust me, you've got power. You owe it to your child and yourself to use it well to the best of your capabilities.

Resisting the Lure of Having Your Child Follow in Your Footsteps
For many parents, they could think of nothing better than to have their kids follow in their professional footsteps. The appeal is strong: the personal validation that comes with having a child say, "Hey, I want to be just like you," along with the seeming promise of cemented camaraderie between you two. These joys are real, assuming that parent and child don't work together and then have a falling out. Trouble arrives when the parent of a college student finds the footstep option so seductive that he makes it his platform. Having a kid follow in your path is only a true compliment if your child travels it with a clear and free conscience.

Why wouldn't your child want to go into your field? Maybe you're an unmatchable role model—a superstar in your field—and your child doesn't want to compete; walking in your footsteps would be more like walking in your shadow. Maybe he senses your professional disappointments and doesn't want to end up there. Maybe he didn't inherit your aptitude in the field; failing a class that's directly related to your parent's work is a particularly shameful experience. Asking a child to enter your field may be like trying to fit a square peg into a round hole; just because you're a round peg doesn't mean your child will be. While he shares characteristics with you, fifty 50 of his inherited aptitudes are different.

Sometimes parents want their children to follow in their phantom footsteps. If parents were forbidden or discouraged from fulfilling their own dreams, then they harbor hope that their child might fulfill it for them. If this rings a bell, now is the time for *you* to fulfill your dream, not your child.

If left to explore free from parental pressures, your child will likely gravitate toward a career path that she is particularly good at and will enjoy. College students tend not to be masochists when it comes to grades; they don't want to continue pursuing subjects in which they get Cs. They get pleasure from getting positive feedback on their abilities. Interfering with your child's natural process of finding her strengths and ultimate pursuit is like blindfolding her, spinning her around, and asking her to swipe at a piñata. Keep reminding yourself that having a positive influence is much more rewarding than having control. Here are some tips for helping your kid get in touch with and follow her instincts.

ACTION
Assisting Your Child's Career Search

1. **Weighing the Pros and Cons.**

   If your child wants your guidance, then:

   a. Ask her questions that will help her sort through her confusion, such as "What do you enjoy and why? What strengths of yours does that area tap into? What are the drawbacks?"

   b. Don't lay your advice down as the law. What's an accurate reflection of the working world today could be quite different from what it will be when your child enters the job market. Even scholarly predictions can be way off. For example, in the 1980s college students were being told to go into academia because many professorial positions would be opening up in the 1990s due to retirement. When the tenured professors retired, many departments retired the positions along with them in order to cut costs. Tell your child the source of the information you provide: an article you read, your own experience, etc. . . .

2. **Finding Other Ways You Can Help.**

   a. If your child is showing interest in your profession, then offer that she observe you at work for a few days to assess the pluses and minuses. Put her in touch with people you know in the fields she's considering. She could conduct informal informational interviews and possibly secure an internship or summer job.

   b. Together, research volunteer or fieldwork positions in the areas she's considering.

   c. If she's a junior or senior and floundering, recommend that she utilize the career counseling services on campus or offer to treat her to a professional career advisor.

3. **Think Comforting Thoughts.**

   a. Remind yourself how grateful you are that your child is in college; a college degree takes a person far no matter what the major. College, regardless of major, prepares students to problem-solve, think flexibly, and work hard: all necessary skills for survival in an ever-changing job market.

   b. A college major will not lock your child into a specific career or keep him locked out of one. In fact graduate admissions often like seeing students with diversified backgrounds. Besides, people who break ground in a field often have an interdisciplinary background.

c. Within a field of study, there are many different career paths. For example, a lawyer can go into politics, administration, or environmental, corporate, public interest, litigation, entertainment, or intellectual property law. These types of decisions are usually made on the graduate or post-graduate level.

Social Life

College students face many social challenges: making brand-new friends, getting along with roommates and dormmates, keeping in touch with high school friends, negotiating the dating maze, handling romance and sex, managing peer pressure to drink, and deciding whether or not fraternities and sororities are for them.

Making Friends

Are you worried that your child won't make enough friends or that the friends he does make will be a bad influence? Getting adjusted socially in college is an odd task—terrifying and thrilling all at once. What helps to break down the barriers and ease the terror is that everybody is new to the place. Students want desperately to connect, so eventually they find a way to. All your child needs is one or two solid friends and she's set.

While high school social life can be ruthless with tight-knit cliques and pressure to conform, in college there's much more freedom. Students make friends in classes, in the dorms, in extracurricular activities, in the dining halls, and at parties; exclusive groups, such as fraternities and sororities, are entirely optional. Usually there's a comfortable place for everyone; it may just take some time for your child to find her niche.

Because college student bodies tend to be more diverse than those in high school, students have more freedom to be themselves.

Some parents worry that their kid will find a place—the wrong place: "At home he was protected. At school, will he fall into the hands of bad company?" Remember, by the time your child reaches college he's already lived eighteen years of his life forming an identity. Odds are against his undergoing any major transformation now unless he ends up on *The X Files* and has an alien transfusion. What were his friends like in high school? If he hung out with a fast-running crowd back then, then he might do so again, yet he also might feel that he's already sowed his wild oats and is now ready to calm down a little. If your child has wild oats that still need sowing, then in all likelihood he'll find kids that he has something in common with in addition to the desire to party. Studious kids party too. College is about exploring your identity, not shedding your old one and trying on a brand-new one.

You may find yourself feeling threatened by the prospect of your child forming attachments to people in her new second home. Your feelings of ambivalence about your child settling in will not elude her emotional radar. She'll sense your conflict and may unconsciously abide by not allowing herself to enjoy the potential friendships around her. Remember, the happier she's feeling in her friendships at school, the more joy she'll bring into her relationship with you.

If your child is clinging tightly to old high school friends, she may be relying on them as transitional objects, much as a kid carries around a security blanket or teddy bear when starting preschool. In all likelihood, as she becomes more comfortable in her new surroundings, she'll shift more and more of herself over to school and relegate seeing old friends to vacation time. If this doesn't happen, then you may find that your child is a regular weekend visitor.

Another factor that can slow down a student's adaptation to college is coming from a culture that is underrepresented at a school. An ethnic minority student may wonder, "Where do I fit in here?" Many universities have special programs or student-run clubs that bring students of similar backgrounds together. Even so, some students don't like identifying themselves by their ethnicity; they'd prefer to be integrated into the school as a whole. Prejudice can exist on campus, especially since many students come from small, homogeneous hometowns. Problem-solve with your kid about what he can do to feel more a part of campus life. If you've had experiences with feeling marginalized, share how you coped.

The parents who live in smaller towns are often wondering what it will be like for their child to be exposed to people from so many different cultural and religious backgrounds:

Lynn, a mother: When we saw the diversity of people walking on campus and on the city streets, we were kind of worried about it at first. But now we see it in a more positive sense—it makes the student grow and mature faster because he knows that real life can have many different types of people.

Many concerned parents eventually come to see the diversity as a factor that strengthens, not weakens, their child's character.

Living with Others

Are you worried about how your child will be getting along with his roommate and other people in the dorm? Living with strangers can be the best experience of your child's life, especially if the strangers turn into the closest of friends. Yet, it can also be a nightmare; visitors in and out of his room all the time, nothing remains where he left it, stereo blasting at all hours—you know, similar to how you might have felt having your child at home.

Learning how to negotiate roommate disagreements can prepare your child better than anything for life in the real world. Getting along with others—especially when you have to but don't want to—is a key skill in life. After all, you do want him to settle down eventually and have a family of his own. What better way to learn how to live with a romantic partner than to practice on a roommate beforehand, not to mention the fact that most professional environments require forced cooperation.

If your child is having roommate troubles, then the temptation as a loving parent is to come to the rescue. You want to call the resident dorm advisor, the dean, whoever it takes to get your child comfortable in his surroundings. Unfortunately, this would only serve to make your child feel infantilized. What you can do is role-play with him about how to resolve the roommate conflicts.

Although students can file for housing changes, many would rather stay put and tough it out, partly because they may have already developed close friendships in the dorm. You may not always agree with the decisions your child makes, but do try to understand where he's coming from. Keep in mind that college students are resilient, managing all sorts of odd and un-favorable living situations. Overcoming a certain degree of misfortune can make him stronger in the long run.

Maybe your child is getting along just fine in the dorms, but you're the one who's unhappy; co-ed living is not what you had in mind for your child:

Marcus, a dad: *I couldn't believe that boys and girls live on the same floor and pee next to each other. It happened to me. I was at the dorm visiting, and I walked across the hall to a bathroom, and this girl walked in right next to me and went to the bathroom. Why is that necessary? I don't think it's normal in our society. We all make our sounds, which guys don't appreciate from one another. I'm sure girls make sounds too, but they don't need to know about ours.*

Not only do the majority of parents come to terms eventually with the concept of co-ed living, they may also come to see it as an advantage:

David, a dad: *The dorm she ended up with was co-ed, and it was just like a little kibbutz. They really supported each other. When my daughter would go into the city with girlfriends, they would always grab one or two of the guys so they'd have males with them when they went. It was just great.*

What other benefits of co-ed living can you think of? What fears does it bring up? Sex might be what comes to mind first.

Sex

Odds are that college students are going to have sex, whether they live with members of the opposite sex or not. These days, many junior high and high school students are already having sex. The real question in to-day's world isn't "Is my college-aged child having sex?" but rather, "Is she having safe sex with somebody who treats her well?"

There's something about the thought of your child having sex that can bring on an automatic shudder of "Oh no!" Take a moment now to really examine your objection; delve underneath any sense of moral concern you have and ask yourself what do you think would happen to your child if she has sex. Is it concern that she'll be emotionally destabilized? Vulner-able to being hurt? Is it that you fear your child contracting a sexually transmitted disease (STD) or becoming pregnant? Or is it mostly just the thought of her doing something that seems so adult? Especially something that maybe you have never been comfortable with yourself? Perhaps secretly you wish you had had more sexual freedom at her age and are jealous.

It's a myth that talking with your child about sex will make him do it.

Resisting change by trying to keep your kid a child will only make her want to initiate herself into adulthood all the more. So you're feeling powerless, you say. Quite the contrary. The biggest sway you still have over your child is the ability to offer good advice that she might hear. Advice that begins with, "I understand that you may be curious about sex and exploring. I just want to mention a few things you might want to watch out for" will get you an audience. If you come across as trying to dissuade her from sex altogether, then she'll not only tune you out, but will also enter sexual relationships with a lot of guilt. With guilt on the mind, she's more likely to approach sex irresponsibly because part of her will try to deny that she's even doing it. The action tips provide some ideas on discussing sex with your child. The notion that talking about sex will spur your child into doing it is a myth.

Also, if you face up to the fact that she's probably having sexual relationships, then you create the type of parent-student relationship where she can turn to you if she's having trouble. Do keep in mind, though, that it's healthy for your child to maintain realms of privacy.

Romance

Now that the topic of sex is out of the way, there's another issue that's at the top of some parents' minds—relationships. "Will she get too serious too fast and cut off all her other options? Will she become so attached that she puts a man before her education and career? Will she wind up living with a man before she even graduates? Will she become devastated if a break-up occurs?"

Sure, some college students meet the love of their life and get serious, but many use the time to explore, even if that's not what they think they're doing at the moment. Take your child's excitement about romance seriously, but not so seriously that you panic. Odds are that this one romantic partner will not be *the* one forever, but you never know—the person could be. There's no one right route to happiness in this world. Believe me, if somebody had discovered it, everyone would be running to follow suit.

Is it possible that your child could end up living with a romantic partner sooner rather than later? In today's "anything goes" atmosphere, yes. The good news is that there is no longer a stigma on young people who decide to live together without getting married. Besides, it gives people the opportunity to have a trial union, saving themselves the grief that can come from feeling forced into a marriage too soon. Since you were raised in different times, accepting this new philosophy can be difficult. Just think about yourself, your relatives, and friends: Might their futures have turned out any brighter if they had had this option?

If your resistance to your child falling in love is particularly strong, then perhaps you're worried that this would signal the ultimate loss of your child's love: Trust me, hearts are big; they have plenty of room for both romantic and parental devotion. Romantic love can even expand the heart, making more room for familial affection. Seeing your child bubbling over with hopeful excitement might also stir up your own feelings of romantic disappointment; remind yourself that you still have options.

If you're an immigrant parent, your deepest wish may be for your child to marry a person from the same cultural background. You hope in your heart of hearts that she'll carry on the family traditions that have meant so much to you over the years. While you may fear acculturation, choosing to raise a family in America means that there aren't just pressures on your child to date the people around her; there are also temptations.

Growing up in the U.S., she sees herself as having as much, if not more, in common with the boy down the hall as she does with the son of your friend. It's like raising your child in a candy store and saying, "Sorry, no sweets." If you pressure your Americanized child to comply with your wishes, she will more likely sneak around behind your back and dodge you altogether. When keeping your child connected to your culture is of primary concern, then make sure to celebrate the holidays and gently point out that the university has cultural courses and clubs. Also, cook her favorite ethnic dishes when she visits. Beware, one thing for certain not to do is to invite your friend's son of similar background to the meal without asking your daughter's permission first.

Sexual Orientation

College is an important time for students to understand their own sexuality. For students who are homosexual or bisexual, high school is often too insular an environment for them to come out, so they usually spend those years passing themselves off as straight. In the hometown, everyone knows them, from the next-door neighbors, to the school principal, to the local grocer. Being at a university means being in a more anonymous setting. This is not to say that there isn't homophobia and prejudice on college campuses; there certainly is. But it is still often a safer place for gay and lesbian students to find comfort and strength in each other.

It's estimated that 10 percent of the total population demonstrates a sexual preference for people of the same sex. Do you think your child might be homosexual? If so, it's of the utmost importance that you look inside yourself and find a way to embrace who he is. He's probably had some inkling of his leanings since he was a young boy going through puberty. He has no choice as to his orientation. If he did, he would probably choose to be straight simply because it's much easier to take the path of least resistance in this society. He is not doing this to hurt you.

Remember, college doesn't change a person's sexual orientation, it just helps her come to terms with who she is and, hopefully, celebrate her sexuality. Your acceptance is key in this process and could actually save her life; the population subgroup that has one of the highest suicide rates in this country is homosexual and bisexual teens.

Is It All Greek to You?

What do most universities have that most high schools do not? Fraternities and sororities. People have wide-ranging attitudes about the university Greek system. Some parents and students think that they are the best thing to come along since refrigeration:

Brenda, a mother: *The fraternity helped my son adjust. He's not only spending time with young men of his age, but it's also the gentleness; they don't make fun* *of each other; they don't take advantage of each other; they just help each other, and that is very, very, very nice. The brotherhood really has some meaning in that particular fraternity. They have each other to work and study with—something my son didn't like to do much, but he was trained because of the brothers.*

Others view them more as bars than homes:

Says a father, **Richard,** *who himself looks back fondly on his old fraternity days: Nowadays you walk down fraternity row and it smells like a brewery.*

Despite the attempts of some universities to regulate the amount of drinking and drugging that goes on in the Greek system, partying is rampant, along with peer pressure to participate. However, each house has a particular personality and approach to partying, which ranges on a scale from megadrinkers to weekenders to teetotalers. Your child is likely to fall in with the crowd that best matches his own attitudes. While I don't recommend trying to stop your child from rushing, you can talk with him about responsible drinking.

The rush period is incredibly stressful, especially if the student has just arrived on campus. The process of putting oneself under the scrutiny of a bunch of strangers can lead to a massive dose of insecurity. Nonetheless, it's your child's choice if she wants to undergo the bidding process. Many students enjoy the socializing that rush brings. The best you can do is be there to support her, letting her know how wonderful she is independent of the outcome. If she fails to gain acceptance to a house, send comforting thoughts her way: "They want people who conform to a specific mold; you're too special and unique for them."

If you were a member of a certain sorority or fraternity, you may be jumping up and down with excitement over the prospect that your child will continue the tradition. The torch can only be carried if your child shares your enthusiasm. Cozy up for a little photo reminiscing and offer to attend a postfootball party together. Other than that, the ball's in your child's court. Maybe he'll expand your horizons by joining a drama club or orchestra.

Illicit Substances

One popular way that college students manage their social anxieties is by drinking or getting high. Marijuana is the drug most commonly used by college-aged kids. The majority of college kids are too young to drink legally, yet alcohol is integral to most social activities on campus. Students gather for happy hour after classes—for a beer. They go to a party to flirt and dance—they drink to loosen up. They go to a football game to cheer on their home team—drinking is part of the zealous spirit. Although some campuses are attempting to crack down on drinking and to create non-alcoholic social alternatives, drinking remains rampant:

Felicia, a mother: Roy said that for his first semester there were a lot of kids that had never had any independence and they got ripped when they got over there. And Roy felt that he didn't need to do that because he had already had a lot of freedom in high school.

If your child didn't have the chance to discover how much she can drink before the room starts spinning or before she vomits, then college will likely be the time for these wondrous discoveries.

The reassuring fact is that while the majority of college students engage in some form of illegal substance use, the majority of them emerge from their experimental phase intact in mind, body, and soul. They also graduate and become productive adults. Did you ever experiment with substances? Did your friends? Can you honestly say that you've never lost control, even just a little?

Rather than the question being, "Will my child use alcohol or drugs?" it becomes, "How responsibly will my child handle these substances?" Does your child tend toward the sensible side or is he prone toward excess? Did you have any discussion about drugs and alcohol when she was living in your house? What type of role model have you been? It's never too late to convey the important facts. The action on the next page will help you talk about using controlled substances in moderation. Advising only the abstention route will likely shut down her hearing system (unless addiction runs in the family).

ACTION
Assisting Your Child's Social Adjustment

1. **When Your Child Is Struggling to Make Friends, Here's What You Can Do.**
   a. Comfort your child by reminding him of the close friends he made back home and why he's so likable. Point out that he's not the only student who's trying to get his courage up to meet new people.
   b. Recommend that in the beginning of school he make an effort to attend the orientation events, no matter how corny they may seem. Joining clubs, attending special lecture events and open houses, participating in a gym class, signing up for smaller seminar courses, volunteering in the neighboring community, taking a social dance class, even taking a part-time job in sales on campus are all ways to meet people. Having something in common is a great excuse to start talking. All it takes is an ounce of recognition from a class, an activity, or a gathering to spark a conversation and perhaps a future friendship.
   c. If after a few months your child isn't finding a social niche, then a few sessions with a counselor on campus might help him figure out what's preventing him from making friends.
   d. If he's not clicking with the other students, then maybe he and the school are a mismatch. Certain colleges do attract certain types of kids. A transfer may be in order.

2. **Advising Your Child on Sex.**
   Did just reading this heading make you blush? Even if you're red in the face for the entire conversation, it's good to have a chat. Obviously, we're not talking about the birds and the bees basics. It's all about emphasizing the importance of her feeling safe emotionally and physically. Tell her she might already know everything you're going to say, but that it would help you sleep better if she lets you get it out.
   a. She should listen to her gut instincts, as opposed to any type of peer pressure, when it comes to sex. It's her body—her domain.
   b. HIV can be transmitted through oral, anal, or vaginal sex. Latex condoms are the only form of protection against the HIV virus, which leads to AIDS. Say you've heard that flavored condoms for oral sex don't taste that bad. But you don't have to go as far as recommending the chocolate. Periodic HIV tests are a good idea for any sexually active person.

c. When using condoms, it's a good idea to have a back-up form of protection, the birth control pill or diaphragm for example, because condoms can break or slip off.

d. Because there are plenty of other dangerous STDs—including ones that can threaten one's fertility or cramp one's love life—she should visit the university gynecological services at least annually and call them with any specific questions she might have. Health insurance through the university is a good idea. If she seems curious to learn more now, buy her a book (see Appendix).

e. Brainstorm with her on how to best prevent date rape. Make sure to include in the discussion how being intoxicated makes you more vulnerable. If you have a son, help him see how it's his responsibility to make sure that the woman he's involved with feels safe and secure. A "No" from a woman at any point in the sexual process means "Stop" for the guy.

f. She should know that if at any point she has an experience in which she feels that somebody has taken advantage of her against her will, rather than be silenced by shame, she should be assured that she is innocent. Tell her that she should seek counseling to cope with the trauma and that she can always turn to you.

g. Let her know that if she's homosexual, she has your support.

h. During your talk, don't expect or request any reply. Even if your child's only response is nodding her head and rolling her eyes, she hears what you're saying. Underneath her cool exterior, she's fascinated and impressed that you got your courage up to broach the topic so frankly.

3. **Think Your Child Might Be Depressed?**

a. Assess if your child is:

____ Eating less than usual?

____ Sleeping much more or much less than usual?

____ Having trouble concentrating?

____ Low on energy?

____ Having little interest in her usual activities?

____ Getting down on herself and her abilities?

b. Of course you need to take external circumstances into account, such as staying up all night to study or not eating because she's nervous about an exam. Also, you're probably wondering how you can answer these questions when you and she are miles apart. First, mull over in your mind the last several conversations you had compared to the ones when you weren't so concerned about her. Any clues? Second, ask her outright, "Have you lost your appetite? Has it been especially hard for you to get out of bed?" You get the idea.

c. If you conclude that your child might be depressed, don't panic. The counseling center on campus is fully prepared to deal with this possibility. Depression is not an uncommon reaction to major transitions; your child needs help adapting. Besides, there may be a more serious problem lurking that can finally receive much-needed professional attention.

4. Advising Your Child on Alcohol and Drugs.

a. Ask your child what dangers he's already wary of and what precautions he takes. Discuss the need-to-know issues: drinking and driving, binge drinking, alcohol poisoning, the proof of different alcoholic beverages, the disinhibiting effect of intoxication, the stripping away of natural instincts for detecting danger, and the fetal position that prevents somebody from choking to death on his own vomit. Make sure to include that because drugs are unregulated, accidental overdosing is easy and the drugs are often laced with dangerous substances. If these concepts aren't familiar to you, then do some research on the Net or in a bookstore and pass the information along (see Appendix). If you see parts of your kid's personality that you think would make him more vulnerable to drinking a dangerous amount or getting into dangerous situations, then point these out. If you've learned some lessons the hard way, share your stories. Let him know that you're available anytime for further consultation on the subject, and that if he feels out of control, he can come to you.

b. If you truly believe and act on the notion that abstention is best, you can say this to your child. Do add that while this is a strong wish of yours, it's probably unrealistic. If he expresses interest in this route, let him know that there are college students who do abstain. Then, work on peer pressure resistance strategies.

c. Most college students drink without becoming alcoholics. If substance addiction runs in the family, he is at risk. How do you know if your child is becoming addicted to alcohol or drugs? If you're concerned, vary the time of day of your calls and determine whether or not he tends to sound intoxicated early in the day, or has been drinking or getting high alone. Have his grades been sliding downwards? When you see him in person, plan an active day that doesn't involve alcohol, and see if he can stay sober.

d. How to act on serious concerns? Tell your child that he hasn't been sounding like himself lately. You miss the warm and funny him. You're concerned that he's unhappy and depending on alcohol. Recommend that he check out services on campus or in the community. You can call the university anonymously to find out what these are. If you have strong evidence that he has a serious problem, consult an expert on conducting an "intervention." It's a way of letting him know that his "secret" is out and that the people in his life love him way too much to stand around and watch him destroy himself.

Finances

Financially supporting a child through college is a mammoth accomplishment. Tuition costs are rising at a rate of 6 to 7 percent, which is *twice* the rate of inflation. Add on the cost of room, board, textbooks, and keeping up with technology, including laptop computers, cell phones, beepers, and CD players. Government assistance seems harder to come by these days, especially if you're earning just enough money to keep your child out of the "in need" category. Many parents work overtime or two jobs just to earn enough to send their children to college. Most kids know that supporting their college education is not an easy task.

With your child being your biggest emotional and financial investment in life, you want to do what you can to help her succeed on the road toward financial independence:

Thomas, a father: *As a parent, I don't worry about having my son make money now—school is his job. I just want him to study and eventually that will prepare him for a productive life later on. That's the key point of education: You want your child to stand up on his own feet—for him to become independent financially. It's something that you hand on to the next generation.*

In some families, the parents are able to cover all their children's college expenses. Other families depend entirely on a combination of loans, scholarships, and work-study. While many families fall somewhere in between these extremes, most kids understand that as a parent you're doing the best you can to ease their burden. It's not how much financial support you give your children that counts; it's your motivation that matters. The essential ingredient to a beneficial financial plan is making sure that it's based on practical necessity, as opposed to your emotional needs.

The key to successful financial college planning is staying objective.

Leaving Room for Independence

Money can be a messy matter that taps into people's hopes and fears. There are people who have a ton of money and spend it all. Then there are those who have little money and make it last. Some people have more than enough money to survive and thrive, yet live in fear that they'll end up in poverty. Then there are people who have less money, but relax and enjoy life.

Where do people develop their attitudes about money? From their families growing up. Think about your own approach to money. What money messages did each parent send you? Are you thrifty or extravagant? Are you calm or anxious? How about your spouse? Who does your college-aged child take after?

A college student can live entirely on her parents' money and feel dependent, resentful, and beholden. Or she can feel competent, grateful, and independent. What makes the difference? Your child's personality plays a role, but the most powerful factor is how you arrange the financial details and the messages you send.

The best strategy is to deposit a lump sum of money in your child's personal bank account each semester to be used for books, entertainment, and living expenses. The key point here is that the child is free to spend as she sees fit. Change assister parents do not monitor the withdrawals and purchases because they see this an opportunity for their kids to learn about money management within a semi-protected environment. They do, however, set implied limits. The child knows that she is expected to make the money last and can't use it to purchase large luxury items, such as a motorcycle or a deluxe cell phone. They give their kid leeway to learn from her own mistakes. If money is tight in the family, then the leeway room may be a little less than in those families where there's financial breathing room:

Marshall, a dad: I think that my son's perception of monies and what it takes to have what he has is a little distorted right now. He's not totally aware of how much he spends and how it goes. But he seems to be learning over time how to keep better track of his spending.

Some college students learn money management skills better by being given a lot of freedom, while others blossom more fully when given independence in smaller increments. Change assister parents try to tune into their child's rhythm and teach him financial skills accordingly.

Giving your child room to learn from his own mistakes is a good way to teach money management skills.

Change Resister Pitfalls Change resister parents give their children as much financial support as they are capable of, but tend to monitor their child's spending on a regular basis and in sharp detail:

Jasmine, a student: The credit card I have now is on my parent's account. So when I charge something, they say, "Why did you think that we would pay for this?" Then there's this whole rigamarole where I say, "I'll write you a check to make up for it." Then they say, "No, no, it's okay. It's just the principle of the matter.

The unfortunate result of having your child account for all money spent is that she loses confidence in her own abilities and feels that she can't enjoy her journey toward full adult status. Your child has very little incentive to improve her money management skills because she doesn't have the independence to utilize them.

If you find it tempting to monitor your child's spending on a regular basis, then take the time now to consider why. The thought process motivating your behavior may be more unconscious than conscious at this point. Is it because you fear that your child might not need you anymore, so you cling to money as the glue holding the family together? While this is understandable, it will have the opposite effect of the one intended; she'll feel that you mistrust her, and become emotionally distant. In addition, she'll probably jump at the first chance she gets to become completely financially independent; even if it's to the detriment of her career path.

Another possible motivator for keeping your child on a tight financial leash may be because you are genuinely concerned that she can't handle finances. College students exhibit a wide range of money management abilities—from saving more than parents could ever have dreamed of to spending money right and left until nothing remains.

Let me ask you: Haven't you ever taken $100 out of the ATM and then four days later wondered where it had all gone? You search through your pants and coat pockets like mad looking for the money. You think to yourself, "It's impossible that so much could have disappeared so fast. Was I robbed and I didn't know it? Did I give the cleaners a twenty instead of a ten by accident?" while all along, you had already spent the money. And all of this is after years of practice!

If your child is bad at keeping track of her spending, of course you shouldn't simply open your wallet and let it run dry. But you should also avoid employing guilt induction or scare tactics:

Bob, father who works as a policeman: *My daughter picked up a $90 library fine that I had to pay. "A $90 fine!" I said. "Do you know how many hours I had to work, risking my life and limb"—very dramatic about that— "for you to pay a library fine?" She got the message. I still pay the library fines. I still pay the phone bills. I still pay the clothing bill. So, not a problem.*

A parent-child relationship with little or no guilt on both sides leaves more room for positive affection. The actions that follow will help you guide your child along the path of responsible money management and preserve the affection in your bond.

Keeping Money and Emotional Issues Separate

Change assisters often have a knack for making finances straight-forward, objective, and concrete for their children, which is especially important when the family doesn't have a comfortable financial cushion to fall back on:

Lynn, a mother: Before she went to school she told us roughly how much money she has from her scholarships, then she set a goal of how much she wants to make. And then we told her how much we want to give her. So, it's some kind of contract, very nicely worked out. She's happy, and we have flexibility that we try to give her one way or another when something doesn't go exactly according to plan.

Even when the family has college costs well covered, it helps kids to know this because they are wondering, "Am I a burden?" If you have a nest egg put aside explicitly for funding your child's college education, then by all means, tell him so. As a student said, "It's comforting to know that the money for my education isn't coming out of my parent's current wages." If you haven't been fortunate enough to have been able to put money aside, don't flog yourself, every parent does the best she can.

Avoid Attaching Any Strings Change resister parents are so fearful of losing all influence over their kids that they often give into the temptation of making financial support conditional. The most common arrangement is to connect the amount of money provided to how well the student performs academically:

Adam, a student: If I'm messing up, then my parents would say, "You should study a little bit more." Then they'll cut my allowance. If I get an A, my dad will give me $20.

Anita, a mother: We bribe her. If she gets good grades we're going to help her buy a car.

By bribing their children, these parents turn learning into a means to an end. You might be thinking, "But isn't that what a grading system does anyway?" To a certain extent grades may drive performance, but in a stimulating academic atmosphere, the desire to expand one's realm of knowledge can play an important role. Yet, if parents are reinforcing a university's policy of emphasizing grades as the ultimate sign of achievement, then the odds are quite low that the child will come to appreciate knowledge for its intrinsic value; it's the desire to learn and build skills that are the underpinnings of a successful career and happy life.

The other major problem associated with interconnecting monetary support and grades is that this plan could backfire entirely. When an academic challenge becomes really rough, your child will be too detached from the subject to stick with it and struggle through. In addition, rather than keep your child close, you could wind up pushing him away:

Joseph, a father: I used to threaten him that if he didn't get good grades I wouldn't support him. But now I haven't seen his grades, because he doesn't show them to me anymore.

While change assisters don't attach monetary meaning to grades, they do draw a reasonable line that usually doesn't have to be vocalized because their kids aren't coming close to crossing it—that line being failing most classes due to lack of effort. As one father said, "As long as my son is putting out a fair effort, I'll support him. My backing isn't at all based on his abilities." These parents focus their energies on helping their kid gain academic assistance.

Change assisters believe in the concept of positive reinforcement, but they use means that foster learning—their confidence, pride, and interest. A child doesn't need a good grade to earn this form of reinforcement— demonstrating effort is enough:

Richard, a dad: Every time my kids got their report cards, we'd go out for ice cream no matter what the grades were. I always thought it's hard on children when they get their report cards, whether they're good grades or bad. I figured, you did the best you could, or if you didn't, now you know you didn't. That's the end of that now—you can start all over again. So let's go have ice cream.

How would you translate this nurturing parental tradition to the college period? Remember, no matter how cavalier your child sounds about receiving his grades, he's not feeling that way.

Another major pitfall that parents fall into is warning that poor academic performance will lead to moving back home. This admonition makes little sense because commuter students who live at home against their true wishes have lower G.P.A.s than students who live in the dorms. Financial backing of housing shouldn't be used as a punishment/reward system. Remember, if your child desires to live at school, it will benefit all of you to do whatever you can within reason to accommodate.

Refrain from making financial support contingent on your child's behavior and achievements.

Letting Your Child Contribute If S/he Desires

Another financial arena in which family dynamics get played out is in the struggle over whether or not the child will gain part-time employment. In some instances, parents want their child to work, but the kids don't want to. The opposite also occurs:

Sarah, a student: *Sometimes I feel kind of guilty asking my parents for extra money. I feel like if I had a job, then I wouldn't have to impose on them as much for my extra things. So sometimes there's a little resentment in the fact that they don't want me to have a job.*

If the child goes ahead and gets a job against parental wishes, the parent might throw another block:

Lori, a student: *When I get a job and save money in my account, my dad never wants me to use my money. Sometimes I want to use my own money and I feel like he's not letting me. He monitors the amount in my account to make sure I'm not taking any out. If I do, then I need to ask him first and he needs to know what I'm using the money for. He wants to make sure that I'm saving and not buying stuff that I don't really need.*

The desire to have your child put money into a savings account and focus her energies on school work are nurturing goals. When parents go way beyond their child's wishes to achieve these aims, then there's unspoken motivation. Parents fear that if their child starts earning her own money, then, "That's it—she won't need me at all." What's a healthy way of handling a child who's champing at the bit to work but you'd prefer she concentrate on school? Here's the most common resolution:

Keith, a student: *I'd like to work, but my parents want me to just concentrate on school, especially this first semester. So I'll just keep going with it, and not worry about it right now. They said that I could always get a job next semester.*

These parents figure that by the time the second semester rolls around, their son will have a better sense of higher education's demands and be better able to make an informed decision about whether or not he can handle work on top of school. Here are additional tips on how to approach finances objectively.

ACTION
Taking the Emotions Out of Finances

1. **Be Aware of Your Own Money Madness.**
   a. Ask yourself whether or not you're fearful of losing your child. If so, then be extra alert for signs of reliance on money as family glue.
   b. Get in touch with your own money hang-ups and try not to let them interfere when planning your child's finances. If you've inherited certain money issues from your parents, then take pride in trying to break the intergenerational chain now by not passing them along to your child.
   c. If you went to college, what were the financial arrangements made and how did you feel about them? Was it an experience you liked and want to replicate for your child or one you'd like to spare him of? If you find yourself jealous of the fact that your child can have an easier go of it than you had, then address these feelings yourself so that they don't sabotage your current financial planning.

2. Devise a Concrete Plan.

a. Calculate the costs of college tuition, room and board, books, utilities, health insurance, activity fees, transportation, clothing, and entertainment. If there's a car involved, then there's insurance, registration, repairs, and gas. Get whatever figures you can from the university. Once you've computed a figure, add a little to it. One of the unfortunate rules of thumb for life is that living costs more than you expect.

b. Determine your family's economic reality. Include a spouse in this exercise. If you are separated or divorced, it's important that you and your ex communicate clearly on this topic. This may mean both of you sitting down with a third party, such as an accountant, to review the situation. Decide what percentage of the cost you can afford to finance without making your life miserable or mortgaging your home; your child isn't going to be happy if you're making yourself unhappy, especially if it's for his welfare.

c. Sit down with your child and significant other and collaborate on devising a realistic, detailed plan. Examine the pros and cons of loans, scholarships, grants, work-study, and your child getting a part-time job. To learn more about these options, speak with the financial aid department at your child's school, or visit the "College Guides" section of your largest local bookstore and peruse the books on financing a college education until you find one you like. Surf the Internet for sites guiding you to special scholarships and loans. (See Appendix for list of books and web sites.)

d. Build in flexibility. There needs to be some leeway to purchase unnecessary items like music albums, a new sweater, and a meal at a restaurant, and to see movies, and have fluctuating telephone and cell phone bills. Decide what steps you all will take if unexpected costs arise or your child fails to stay within the anticipated budget. Figure out what you will do if your child actually ends up with extra money in his account at the end of the semester. If you let it stay where it is, your child will have more incentive to watch what he spends if he gets to keep what's left over.

e. Use adult terminology. You want your child to feel like he's maturing into an independent adult, even if it is still on your money. For example, you used to give your child an "allowance" every week or month; now you give him a "stipend" every period.

f. Open up a personal bank account for your child near the university. A checking/savings account that provides checks as well as an ATM card that also doubles as a credit card is preferable. Decide when you will deposit lump sums in the account; at the beginning of each semester is preferable. In addition, some universities offer students the option of setting up special accounts that can be used specifically for spending on campus.

g. Check in with your child. Every now and then ask your child, "Do you have everything you need? Would more money help?" Your kid may be coming up short, but feels too embarrassed or guilty to ask you directly for what she needs.

3. Consider All Angles of the Job Question.

a. Perhaps your kid is itching to work when you don't want him to. Or maybe he has no interest in working, when you feel the family needs the money. Keep in mind that college can be high-stress; some kids can handle a job on top of school work better than others; and students who are members of a sports team or theatre troupe may find it literally impossible to add on a part-time job.

b. Your child's earning potential is very low right now. Being a college graduate is the ticket to higher pay.

c. Non-paying internships or volunteer positions are typically much more relevant to a student's future plans than jobs are. These experiences can help guide her career choices, give her professional contacts, as well as the experience she needs to apply to graduate programs or paying positions. Many times what begins as volunteer work turns into a paid post down the line.

4. Teach Your Child Money Management Skills.

a. Tell your child it's not that you don't trust her; it's that you think every college student could benefit from a crash course. Run through the basics of: balancing a checkbook; withdrawing and depositing money using an ATM machine; using a credit versus debit card; and calculating the charges that accrue when you withdraw on your debit card more money than lies in your checking account, or don't pay your credit card bill on time.

b. If your child is handling money irresponsibly, talk with him about how you don't want to have to micromanage his finances. You believe he can do it, but that together you need to figure out how to remedy the current situation. Ask him if there are any practical tools you failed to provide him. This takes some of the burden of blame off of him. He's already feeling ashamed and embarrassed, even if he doesn't show it. If you've determined that his being spoiled is the root cause, then start by taking responsibility: "Perhaps in wanting the best for you, we didn't handle finances all that well. Is it possible that we spoiled you?" This is a terrific opener; see where it leads.

To Students

1. Assert Your Autonomy.

If your parents are the type of worriers who want to come into your life and take over, try this suggested script; you may need to enlist it several times before it has an impact.

    a. Gently assert your independence: "It's time for me to learn the consequences of making my own decisions."

    b. Along with a compliment: "You've prepared me well for the world—I think I can do it."

    c. Elevate and involve them: "You're wise to the world; I would love to hear your opinions."

    d. Reassert that you have the final say: "And I will certainly take your thoughts under advisement."

2. Fight the Temptation to Let Parents Take Over.

Maybe your struggles aren't to get parents off your back, but actually to keep them there. Life's choices can feel weighty and intimidating, so perhaps you're tempted to let your parents decide for you. It's best for you to start honing your own decision-making skills; use college as a relatively protected time to start making your own decisions in a trial-and-error fashion.

3. Take Charge of Your Career Choice.

Here are a few sentiments to vocalize if your parents are trying to influence your choice of major:

    a. "I will take your advice into account. But ultimately, the only way that I will succeed in this world is if I follow my own interests. I know you want me to succeed."

    b. "The way I see it, we have two options: We could continue arguing about my life incessantly and wind up dreading the next time we have to talk to each other. Or we could have a nice conversation and say goodbye wanting to talk again soon."

c. If they persist, say, "Frankly, the more you argue your case, the more it makes me want to do the exact opposite." If they "But, but . . ." you, say, "I'm just telling you how it makes me feel."

d. Hold your ground. While parents will huff and puff, they generally won't blow the house down; in other words, parents tend not to pull out financial support if their child doesn't follow their professional wishes.

4. Taking Tender Loving Care of Yourself.

You are now the proud caretaker of yourself and have everything to gain from doing a good job. Even if parental nagging to be healthy makes you want to be irresponsible, decide to be safe and healthy for your own reasons, not theirs.

a. Implement what you need to feel physically safe, whether it be having a friend escort you back from the library late at night or carrying a whistle.

b. Make sure that you are eating well enough to maximize your brainpower and energy level. Weigh your nutritional balance more toward whole-grain carbohydrates, fruits, vegetables, and protein and iron sources, such as fish, chicken, and beans. Cut down on foods high in saturated fats, such as hamburgers and French fries; but don't eliminate dietary fat altogether—you need some to survive. Don't forget to drink as much as eight glasses of water a day. A once-a-day multivitamin is no substitute for healthy eating, but it can supplement it.

c. If your weight is becoming an obsessive concern, visit the campus counseling center before the worries get out of hand and develop into an eating disorder. The majority of eating disorders begin with a simple diet.

d. Never underestimate the power of a good night's sleep. Being rested not only helps you concentrate better, but also makes you better prepared to fight cold germs and emotional stress. Problems seem much more over-whelming when you're sleep-deprived. Caffeine may give you a temporary energy boost, but it messes with your ability to get the sleep you need. To perk yourself up when exhausted, try the twenty- to thirty-minute power nap.

e. It's inevitable that you'll catch whatever bug is going around at some point. Visit the health services when symptoms don't subside after a few days—why not try to ease your misery?

f. It can be hard to party in college without encountering alcohol, drugs, and cigarettes. If your modus operandi is to abstain, good for you and hold onto this. If you like to participate, then educate yourself on the dangers and let moderation be your guide. When everyone around you is sucking down the alcohol, it can be hard to get a grip on your own limits. While cigarettes are highly addictive and can kill you in the long run, too much alcohol and drugs can kill you on the spot. (See Appendix for further sources of information.)

g. Last but not least, there's safe sex. STDs have been known to run through college campuses like wildfire. In many cases you and/or your sexual partner can have an STD and yet have no clue that you are infected. As you know, the HIV virus that causes AIDS is deadly, but did you also know that HPV (human papilloma virus) can lead to cancer and chlamydia can turn into PID (pelvic inflammatory disease) that causes infertility in females? The best ways to protect yourself are to always use a latex condom—check the expiration date on the condom—with lubrication, and make sure that you and your partner go for regular STD and sexual health check-ups. It never hurts to know a lot. If you have questions that you're reluctant to ask a health educator in person, anonymously consult your campus health services advice line, a national hotline, a web site, or a book (see Appendix for resources).

h. If you find that being away from your home town gives you the freedom to get in touch with any feelings of homosexuality or bisexuality that you have, then make sure to get support for coming out and exploring your sexuality. Counseling services and campus clubs are two potential sources of support, along with the Gay and Lesbian National Hotline (see Appendix).

5. **Avoid Being Overly Compliant with or Reactive Against Parents' Wishes.**

a. Purposely going in the opposite direction that parents tell you to go will backfire; inevitably, you won't be happy and there might even be a parental "I told you so" waiting for you in the wings. Besides, if you make a point of going in the opposite direction, you're actually giving your parents a big say in your life, which is just what you're trying to avoid.

b. Here's something I bet you haven't considered: If you suspect that your parents are very concerned that you won't need them anymore, then you might be helping them to feel needed by unconsciously messing up. This is a complicated psychological process that often takes professional assistance to unravel.

6. Seek Help When You Need It.

Adjusting to college is no easy task. If you're having trouble adapting to the academic demands, figuring out your future path, or finding a social niche, then use these many channels of assistance open to you:

a. Your parents have lived on this planet for many years and may be a source of sound advice. Only you can evaluate how much of an objective help they can be. They would probably love to help, and there is absolutely no shame in asking for it. Why not try knocking on your RA's door and see how her advice rates?

b. If you have questions about your major choice and requirements, then visit your academic advisor; that's what she or he is there for.

c. Struggling with your schoolwork, whether it be a particular subject or study habits in general? Then attend your TA's or professor's office hours, seek tutoring assistance on campus, and consider forming a study group.

d. If social or academic problems persist, then seriously consider consulting a therapist in the counseling center on campus; college adjustment difficulties are their specialty; several sessions should be free of charge.

CHAPTER 8

Change Desisters
How to Keep the Family Together

Conflict in change desister families is so great that family members welcome the separation that college brings. The danger is that they may use this period as a chance to sever ties completely. If this happens, the emotional cost for everybody is tremendous; there's always a huge missing piece in the parents' and child's lives. Without even a sliver of secure parental base to stand on, the college student can have difficulty adjusting to the university.

The good news is that the physical and emotional distance that college provides is the best window of opportunity for positive change that a change desister family can have. It certainly helps that having the child pursue a higher degree is something that the parents can be proud of and even take some credit for. Here's an inspirational story. At the time Sandra left for college, family relationships at home were so tense that the only interaction she had with her parents was in the form of arguments. The departure for college was a welcome relief for everyone. For the first two years of college, the only family contact consisted of obligatory holiday gatherings and a handful of phone calls. Then, something happened:

Sandra, a student: My anger toward my parents started to slip away. The lack of contact and the physical and emotional distance helped me gain some perspective. I didn't need them so much anymore to fill the void in my life; I

had my own apartment, a job, friends, and a boyfriend. My life was progress-
ing, and the anger that I carried around with me about my parents was weigh-
ing me down.

One particular Sunday, I needed to do my laundry, but the washing machine
in my building was broken. I wound up calling my mother to ask if I could
come down to use her facilities. She suggested that my boyfriend and I stay for
dinner. There began the beginnings of a tradition; every Sunday around noon,
my boyfriend and I go to my parents to do laundry, have dinner, and stay
until around 10:00 P.M. This laundry ritual cleared the way for my parents to
see me as an individual and for me to see my parents as human.

Rather than wait and see if your child is going to find a way to recon-
nect, you can take charge of the situation and be the one to reach out.
If you're a change desister parent who is reading this book, then you
clearly want to turn things around in your family. Commend yourself for
being brave enough to face your disappointments and fears of losing your
child. Take comfort in the fact that you are seizing upon an excellent opportunity to give your relationship with your child a rebirth. This action-
packed chapter will help you manage your resentment of how the
relationship proceeded in the past, and work toward a healthier, happier
future. Put together several baby steps in a row and you wind up with giant leaps.

How Did All the Strife Begin?

After your child leaves, you take a deep breath and let out a sigh of relief, then you realize that deep inside are feelings of melancholy and regret that things could've been different. Even though you and your child
have fleeting hopes of reconciliation, neither of you expresses it. You and
he are stuck in a standoff; each of you is sitting in your corner, sticking
by your version of the story of why the relationship isn't working.

Is this a chicken-and-egg question in which you could spend from now
through eternity trying to figure out which of you started this whole mess
or is there actually an answer? In all likelihood, the deep-seated conflict
between you two was probably born out of an unhappiness that you have

in your own life or a pattern that you learned in your own family growing up. When family conflict begins when the children are young, research has found that more often than not, troubled kids are born out of troubled families, as opposed to the other way around.

Think about your own experience growing up; was family life rough or smooth? If it was stressful, why? What was going on with your parents? When did your relationship take a turn for the worse and why? Now ask the same questions of your current nuclear family. How many of the characteristics that irk you about your child can you also see in yourself—the butting-heads phenomenon? Or perhaps you can find these qualities in your spouse or your own parents. Very little about your relationship is accidental. No matter how bewildering it may seem to you, in the scheme of family dynamics it all makes sense.

Let's take an example. In the Serrano change desister family, Mary and her parents resent each other and fight a lot. All family members were looking forward to Mary's departure for college; their only disappointment was that she didn't go farther away to school. According to her parents, the trouble began when Mary's younger sister, Kelly, was born and Mary angrily had to give up some of her only-child turf. This alone, however, wouldn't be enough to cause serious rifts in the family. The parents had to actually favor the newborn child over the firstborn for a period of time in order for Mary to develop deep resentment. Even if Mary had acted out the typical pattern of anger over being "replaced" by a younger sibling, it would have been the responsibility of the more mature parents to demonstrate constant love in the face of their child's seeming rejection. It's that parental burden of having to take the high road again and be the secure base. If the Serranos had done this, Mary would have eventually realized that her fears of losing her parents' love were unwarranted and her upset and irritability would have subsided. Sadly, the Serranos were each going through their own difficult time in their troubled marriage, which made it hard for them to focus on Mary's needs.

As a way of coping with the marital strife, Mrs. Serrano focused a lot of attention on her newborn baby Kelly, who grew up to be her mother's companion. At the same time, Mr. Serrano distanced himself from the whole family. It didn't help matters that Mary had learning disabilities that required much assistance, so that the majority of the attention Mrs.

Serrano did give Mary was focused on Mary's "defects"—defects that Kelly didn't have.

It's well worth your trying to trace the problems back to their roots; this process just might put a few cracks in the protective shell you've built up around yourself when it comes to your child. The more cracks there are, the greater the chance that you will be able to break clown the barriers and have her feel your love.

The following tips are designed to help you bust out of the pattern of mutual mistrust and miscommunication in which you and your child have gotten stuck.

ACTION
Using the Physical Distance to Bring You Closer

Your child may need some time to break away before he's ready to re-connect in a better way. If you try the suggested actions and they don't catch, hold off for a while and then try again. You never quite know when he's likely to be receptive, but he will be eventually if you don't give up.

1. **Mourn the Loss of How You Hoped the Relationship Would Go over the Years.**
   a. Think back to when your child was first born. What hopes and dreams did you have for him and for your relationship? When did things start getting off track and why? Maybe the timing was off from the beginning because you didn't want to have a child at that point in your life. Maybe a parent of yours fell ill and you had only so much energy to devote to caring for your parent and your child. Whatever it was, find a way to forgive yourself and your child.
   b. What relationship qualities would you like to re-ignite between you two and what would you like to change? What were the best times you shared with your child? Why haven't there been more of them? What conditions bring out the best in your relationship? What were the worst times you shared and why did they come about? What types of circumstances are best avoided?
   c. What aspects of yourself do you see in your child that bring out feelings

of affection? Which characteristics do you have in common that make you butt heads?

2. **Make a Peace Offering.**

a. Let your child know how you wish things had been different between you, and how you regret that you two got locked in a destructive miscommunication pattern. Even though you haven't been the world's greatest source of comfort for him in the past, you are going to try very hard to be supportive of him now. You're here for him if he needs you.

b. If you can take responsibility for some things you wish you had done differently, that would certainly help. Saying you're sorry can only make things better. Your child is not going to respond by pointing his finger at you, saying, "I knew it! I knew it!" Also, don't expect him to thank you, let you off the hook, or take some blame onto himself. You are making an offering to him; no response required.

c. Tell him how proud you are that he's going off to college and that you see this as a wonderful opportunity for you both to mend the problems in the relationship. Again, a little self-deprecating humor can help: something like, "I imagine that it might be easier for you to like me if you don't have to put up with my nagging you on a daily basis." Make sure that he knows that you don't expect him to change his approach in the here and now—that these things take time.

3. **Ease the Tension in the Relationship.**

a. Make a place for your child in the family. A common problem among change desisters is that the college student ends up feeling like a guest in his own home when he visits. To counter this tendency:

• Keep his room the same if you can.

• Make sure to extend invitations to all family gatherings, even if you know he can't or won't make it.

• Keep him informed of family happenings, the good and the bad.

b. When your child comes to visit, try to allow him more freedom in accordance with the independence he's gained at school. In change desister families it's important to make the expectations reasonable and explicit in order to minimize conflict. Involve him in the process of determining the new rules. If there is a younger child still at home, make sure that the college student has more privileges in keeping with the age difference.

c. Be on the lookout for fresh opportunities that college offers you two to

connect on new and neutral ground, such as sporting events or an intellectual exchange.

d. Consider going to see an individual, couples, or family therapist.

e. Be patient with yourself and with your child. These are deeply
entrenched behaviors and feelings that you're working on changing. It
can take quite a bit of time and effort to turn the tide, but you can do it
and the payoff will be tremendous.

4. Facilitate Communication

a. Give your child the benefit of the doubt. Examine the underlying
thoughts and motivations behind what you say. Screen out the negative
aspects and communicate the positive. You have everything to gain from
putting your suspicions on reserve. Because your child will be on the
lookout for implied criticism, even with a simple inquiry about how
school is going, it can help to couch it carefully: "I know how strong you
are and how hard you work. I'm just hoping that you're feeling good
about yourself and how things are going at school."

b. Inquire about your child's areas of strength. Most change desister parents
are tuned in more to their child's weaknesses than their strong points. So
get in touch with what your child has the potential to excel in, such as
languages or track and field, and ask how those areas are going. At this
point, it will be hard for your child to hear any guidance you give without suspecting you of insulting or manipulating her. Grounding your advice in her strengths will help minimize this tendency.

5. Assist Your Child in Finding a Surrogate Secure Base.

Foster and don't stand in the way of any special friendships or professional relationships your child naturally establishes with an adult parental figure. Having
the support of other adults will help give her the strength she needs to open up
to you and consider trusting you.

a. If you think that an older relative or friend of yours who lives near the
school could provide parental-type support, get permission from your child
to give the person her phone number. Your child will be suspicious at first.
Attempt to reinforce the fact that this hook-up is for her, not for you.

b. Offer to help pay for psychological counseling. Since the suggestion of
therapy coming from you can easily be heard as, "Go see a counselor to
fix yourself—you're the problem," try saying, "All the family conflict
we've had has to make it harder for you being away at school without a

strong foundation at home behind you. We'd support you, both financially and morally, if you wanted to see a counselor at school." It will be difficult, but very worthwhile for you to add, "I'm sorry that I've been contributing to your struggles and hope to change that in the near future." If you really want to throw in a clincher, say, "I've been considering seeing a therapist myself." This makes you an excellent role model and is proof positive that you're not putting all the blame on her. Then, follow up and find yourself a counselor.

6. Locate the Source of Tension.

Over time the problematic family dynamics have shifted such that the tension is focused on this one child. It's true that the child's departure for college brings a temporary sense of relief, but soon it will become apparent that all your personal problems have not been solved so easily.

a. Try an experiment; you and your spouse agree not to discuss your college-aged child for two whole weeks and see whether or not you end up fighting about other things instead. If you argue anyway, then it's time to give the marriage some focused improvement time. If you don't, then make Thursdays your day to talk about your college-aged child, and avoid the topic as best you can the rest of the time.

b. Emphasize your child's positive contribution to the family and de-emphasize the stress she causes you. For a student to feel like her parents are suffering because of her is severely damaging to her self-esteem. College is a critical time for young adults to explore their identity and make decisions about their futures. In order for them to maximize their potential, they need to be in touch with what they have to offer the world.

To Students

1. Resist Severing All Ties.

a. The fantasy of cutting off your relationships with your parents—going away to college and not coming back—is tempting, but deep inside you know that this would hurt you as much as it would them. What you really desire is to have the relationship repaired.

b. It can be especially heart-wrenching when you hear so many other students chatting with their parents regularly and looking forward to visits home. Even just listening to a friend complain about how his dad is nagging him about his career choice could trigger envy.

c. Don't give up hope. Holding onto hope can be painful, because you continually open yourself up to feeling disappointed. Remind yourself that your living at college opens the door to new family relationship possibilities that could take place anytime during your college career. So in the back of your mind, keep a spark of hope alive.

d. Just because you weren't responsible for the downfall in the first place and don't have the power to make everything better doesn't mean that you can't plant the seeds for a relationship renewal.

2. **Make Small Moves Toward Reconciliation.**

a. Take the high road. Even though you would love for your parents to realize and acknowledge the errors of their ways, you know that they aren't capable of it right now. Lower your expectations of them for the time being. Don't look for them to be friendlier or kinder than usual; simply decide that you're going to make a series of small outreach efforts independent of their reactions. They will probably be suspicious of you at first because of all the mutual mistrust that has built up over the years. With enough time, you're likely to see them coming around.

b. Call your parents once a week just to say hello and ask them how they're feeling; follow up on what you know is going on in the family. Talk about neutral topics, such as how your favorite professional sports teams are doing, or even about the weather if you can't find anything else in common. If your parents ask you questions about life at school, then try to give them the benefit of the doubt that it's out of caring. Share enough information so that they don't feel completely shut out of your life. Consider saying outright, "With me away from home, we seem to be getting on each other's nerves less, so I thought that this might be a good opportunity for us to improve our relationship."

c. When you go home for visits, set aside a little free time in which you simply hang out with them, even if it means following them around the house as they do chores. Offering to help isn't a bad idea. Keep in mind, the goal isn't to try to worm your way into their hearts—that wouldn't work anyway. It's to see if they will meet you halfway on a certain level of maturity, not as equals—you are still their child—but as two parties trying to reconcile their differences.

d. If your parents are physically or sexually abusive, then seriously evaluate the risks versus benefits of direct contact; your health and safety must come first. This might even require intervention by law enforcement. If a parent is severely mentally ill, such as an alcoholic or paranoid-schizophrenic, then you should realistically determine what the absolute best relationship is that you can hope for and strive for that. Seeking therapy on your part will be essential to feeling in charge of your life again.

3. Gather Support.

a. Make contact with older cousins, aunts, uncles, or grandparents. College is excitement and stress all rolled into one and every student can use a good dose of support. Your goal in touching base with extended family is not to drag them over to your side of the family conflict, but to establish positive ties based on where you're going with your own future. It would be particularly nice for you if you have a relative with whom you share an interest, such as music or the medical profession.

b. For the large vacation blocks of time, split them up between being home with your parents and visiting a friend's home. While it may be painful to see how loving your friend's relationships with her parents are when compared to yours, it could be helpful to observe how more functional families relate.

c. Therapeutic support is definitely a good idea. Certainly your parents could use some as well, but all you have control over is getting yourself some assistance. In a change desister family, even a strong child winds up feeling irrational guilt and low self-esteem over how the family relationships have gone. As a college student you have excellent free therapy at your on-campus counseling center. If your school lacks adequate services, then there is always affordable therapy at local community centers or psychological training centers.

CHAPTER 9

Commuter-Student Families
How to Improve Relationships at Home

The vast majority of college students view living at school as essential for the ultimate college experience. Despite this fact, thousands of kids around the country commute to college from home—some because they want to, some because the college is solely a commuter school, some because they have to for financial reasons, and some because their parents want them to; these parents are typically change resisters.

Parents who either encourage or insist that their kids live at home are motivated by a variety of factors. Many of these parents are extremely protective of their children and let their fears of what will happen to their child take over. Others are so anxious about the possibility of their marriage breaking up that they cling to their kids as a go-between and source of comfort. Many simply fear that the parent-child relationship will deteriorate. In some immigrant families, parents want to maintain their cultural tradition of kids living at home until marriage. In rare cases, parents are violent with each other, so that the child stays home in an effort to protect them from harm.

Some parents of commuters express their change resistance outright, while others disguise it as financial concerns. In the end, you can't slip anything by your kids:

Doris, a commuter student: *My mom kind of made it clear that she would rather have me live at home and save money. But if I really wanted to stay at* *school, she would raise the money. It was kind of my choice, but I got the feeling that she'd rather me not live at school. I'm unhappy; she gave me a choice but she's also saying that I really don't have a choice. The illusion of choice mostly. It's like she's saying you can do it, but I don't want you to. She said we can't afford it, but I felt those vibes in her; if I went away she'd be upset, not upset where she wouldn't talk to me, but she'd still not really want me to go.*

Commuter change resister issues are often extremely complex and unspoken. It's no wonder then that kids frequently leave home for a brief period, move back in, leave again, and so on. There seems to be a tug of wills between parent and student. A student may break free only to find that she's worried sick about her parents' well-being, made worse by the added grief that her departure has caused, and so, moves back. Sometimes, parents release the child because they can see that commuting is taking a toll on her scholastic performance. They often add, "If your grades don't improve, then you're moving back home." Under that type of pressure, it's hard for kids to succeed.

It makes perfect sense that if you would miss your child terribly if she left home, that you would want her to stay. Commuting could start to seem like a brilliant idea considering that it saves a ton of money and means that you could watch out for your child and give her tender loving care. You genuinely think that your child will reap the benefits of living at home, not just the home-cooked food and other perks, but also that she'll study better and luxuriate in the refuge from the chaos of college. You figure, your kid is unhappy with the notion now, but once school beings, she'll see the brilliance behind the plan.

Unfortunately, approximately nine times out of ten, students who have to live at home due to parental change resistance are unhappy—being angry at the situation and at their parents, they adjust poorly to college:

Omar, a commuter student: *I would have liked to have gone to a different school because living at home for college is just like high school, except the workload is harder. It's kind of freer rule-wise, but I really hate living at home; it's just the worst thing in the world.*

Student Adjustment Is Poor

When students live at home against their true wishes, it's extra difficult for them to cope with the social and academic stresses that accompany the commuter's life:

Maria, a commuter student: Commuting takes forever. I get up at five in the morning to get into an 8:00 o'clock class. There are a lot of time gaps in between classes. If I lived over here, I would go to my house to study for a little while, but as a commuter, it's basically an hour of blank time. I really want to live on campus. I think my mom understands that now, but this is only after she sees me struggling. I can't go to late classes; I can't go to tutorial sessions; I can't study late with my friends. Instead of worrying about grades I have to worry about getting home safely before it gets dark. It's like an extra load to worry about, like another class if you will. And also, I'm not meeting as many people as I could if I were on campus. The people I do meet, a lot of them hear that you're living at home and they think, "Oh, you're still living with your parents; you're not mature enough to live on your own."

It's not unheard of for students put in this situation to flunk out or develop an eating disorder. Students might also exhibit the adult runaway phenomenon; when the time comes after college to find a job or go to graduate school, they end up going as far away as possible.

Time Spent Together

Whereas most families in which the child leaves home for college report positive changes in family relationships, the vast majority of commuter-student families experience either no change in familial relations, or a turn for the worse. You know all those tiffs you had with your child during the high school years over curfew, chores, how he leads his life, and just the grumpiness that comes with being in each other's way? Well, if he doesn't move out of the house as a tension releaser, then old conflicts are not going to get better. In fact, they're likely to intensify because with the demands of college, your child is even less available to tend to household duties and participate in family activities than he was before. The most common scenarios are that either you never see him, or that you're often in each other's face:

Stephen, a commuter student: My dad will be like, "Oh, I had a hard day at work." And my mom will be like, "Clean up your room, it's all sloppy." And my sister's like, "Oh, I'm on the phone." My dad will ask me to turn down the music and I'll say, "I don't feel like it."

Lou, Stephen's dad: He doesn't seem to have enough time for us anymore. We're rarely home at the same time, and when we are, he's either on the phone, on the books, or is working. During the high school years, we used to have supper together and we talked. Right now, the time he spends with us is very limited.

When commuter-student parents realize that their fantasies don't match reality, frustration is born. A whole new layer of change resistance may develop: "Why can't family life be like it used to be?" Then you may try to recreate the old sense of family togetherness by insisting that your child spend more time with you. The result? Tension in the parent-student relationship.

Even when a child lives at school during the week and visits most weekends, the family relationships improve:

Neal, a former commuter student: We don't fight as much. We don't argue as much. They don't yell at me as much. I don't yell at them as much.

The Information Jam

Commuter kids lack the physical distance from parents that most people their age have. To compensate, many make an extra effort to create emotional space around themselves. One way they do this is by being reluctant to reveal information about their personal lives and activities. Your child's reluctance to communicate is especially hard for you because you see his ups and downs and want to be there for him. Moreover, because he's struggling for independence, he often interprets your concern as interference. In addition, the little talk time you do have is often occupied with mundane questions like "What's for dinner?" and attempts at working out housemate conflicts. There's little time left for finding out how he's doing, let alone having exciting discussions about world affairs.

You witness your kid's comings and goings from the house and, of course, you're curious about what she's up to. You can't help but to worry, "Will she be safe? Get her studying done? Be with nice people?" The problem is that you already know when she's home and when she's not; just this small amount of knowledge can already seem like an invasion because the parents of most of her peers have no clue where their kids are at all. Young adults were designed to want privacy and freedom, while parents were designed to worry. What's the best solution? Having your young adult child live at school. It's no accident that the American culture encourages college-aged kids to leave home.

Are you convinced yet that having your child live at home with you and commute to college is not ideal? Maybe you are but still need to have your child home for financial reasons, or at least until a departure plan is made. The actions will help you evaluate whether or not your commuter situation is due to change resistance, and then how to either plan for departure or make college commuting less of a hardship on your child and your relationship.

ACTION
Reconsidering and Reconfiguring Commuter Family Life

1. Evaluate the Living Arrangements.
   a. Ask yourself why your child is living at home. Have you given any indication, either directly or indirectly, that you desire that she stay? Is there any reason to believe your child would think you needed her company at home, even though she won't say this outright? If the reasons are purely financial, then examine whether there are options you haven't fully explored. You could possibly apply for bigger loans or look into scholarships. Your child might actually adjust better to college doing work-study while

living on campus than if he's living at home and unemployed. If you can only afford a couple of semesters' room and board, then encourage him to make it his first few. Being on campus to make those initial connections can be critical. Sure, it might be hard for him to return home after getting a taste of freedom, but he'll have more friends and a better sense of how college life functions.

b. If the reasons have an emotional component, examine the part of you that wants your child to live at home. Make a list of what you are afraid will happen to you and to your relationship with her if she leaves. Next to each fear, write your counter-fears—comforting thoughts about why your fear will likely not come true, and also what you will do to help yourself if it does.

c. Let your child know that you now see why commuting isn't the best idea. Obviously, you don't want to just kick your child out. Say, "It seems like living at school has a lot to offer and that's really where you should be right now. We love having you here, but I absolutely want what's best for you." Let her know that if she really doesn't like it, she could always move back. Besides, you'll be just a phone call away.

d. Together, work out a timetable for when your child will move out. If your child has stayed very close to home all of these years, then invite him to take small trips away. First an overnight at a friend's at the dorms. Next a weekend away with a school friend who's heading to his parents' house for the weekend. Next encourage him to go on a ski trip with pals. And so on, until he's spending a whole week away at a time. Then, sit down together and plan his living at school.

e. Decide what you would like to have in place for yourself by the time your child leaves to help you cope, whether it be a satisfying job, activities that occupy some of your evening time, dates if you're single, or marriage counseling if your relationship is in crisis.

2. **Maximize Your Child's Sense of Privacy When She's Living at Home.**

a. A personal entranceway is ideal. If you're fortunate to have enough space in your home to give your child her own floor or to turn the shed into a bedroom, then your efforts will go a long way in terms of his positive affection for you. This will help you as well; you will be spared those late nights sitting up in bed trying to listen for the door to open as a sign that he's safely home.

b. A private phone line is practically a must. If this fits within your budget, it would be a big help for your child to have her own line and answering machine. Think of the benefit to you; you don't have to play messenger.

c. Refrain from asking too many questions about her personal life. Connect around personally neutral issues that involve her university, whether it's the college basketball games on TV or how what she's learning relates to the news in the morning newspaper. This shows your respect for her growing maturity and won't register on her antenna for picking up invasion-of-privacy signals.

d. If your child is right under your nose, but is unrevealing, it's quite possible that you will be tempted to snoop around your child's room, bookbag, mail, or phone conversations—but you must resist. Gaining knowledge that you shouldn't have or your child finding out what you've done can be incredibly damaging to your relationship.

e. If you're worried about a particular area of your child's life that she's especially quiet about, then imagine the worst possible scenario, the best possible, and the most likely. Try to find the humor in the contrast between your worst-case scenario and most likely one; the imagination can play mean tricks on us all.

3. Facilitate Your Child's Studies.

The notion of your child scheduling her classes to make the commute more convenient is one of those "sounds-good-on-paper-but-doesn't-fly-in-real-life" concepts. It's hard enough for students to fight the competition to get into the classes they want and need for their majors, let alone arrange their classes around commuting. Here's what you can do to help out.

a. Create quiet zones in the home. If you can block off a portion of the house that's free from TV, stereo, video games, and chatter noise, that's terrific. If not, then ask your child at what hours he likes to study and try to get the rest of the family to read, play board games, or do homework when your college student kid is working.

b. Help ease some of her travel time and hassles whenever you can, without, of course, making your life a nightmare.

• Offer to pick her up late from the campus library or from the train station.

• Consider chipping in for a car if you are able.

• If you can afford it, pay for her taking a cab back from the library late at night during finals and midterms.

- Encourage her to find friends on whose couch she can crash.
- Free her up from as many family outings and chore responsibilities as you can. Give her the chores that have time flexibility like vacuuming. Or just make her in charge of her own space and own things, and ask her to help with the dishes if she joins in the family dinner. Free her of all responsibilities when she has exams.

4. **More Ideas . . .**
   a. Facilitate her social life by letting her know that she's welcome to bring friends over anytime and free to come and go as she pleases.
   b. Let your child know that you understand how wearing commuting can be and how much easier life would be for her if she were on campus. Lighten things up with humor. A little parental self-deprecation couldn't hurt, such as making jokes about how you're not the ideal roommate or Saturday night dinner date.
   c. Avoid any secure base reversals. There your child is, so grown-up, taking college courses, and still at home—it's hard to resist consulting her on all sorts of personal issues, not to mention the fact that she can't help notice that you're feeling upset when you come home from work or if you're not taking good care of yourself. She's going feel like she should try to help. It's very important that you refrain from engaging her as a confidant.

5. **Familiarize Yourself with the American College Experience.**
   a. If the university has a program in which parents can live on campus for a day and sleep in the dorms, then give it a try. Even if you already passed up the option the summer before your child began school, the college will be offering it to next year's incoming parents; see if you can get in on it. Your child would probably be more than happy to hook you up.
   b. Rent a few movies that take place on a college campus, such as *With Honors* and *Good Will Hunting*.
   c. Watch a few episodes of a college-oriented TV show. There's always at least one current popular series that takes place on a college campus.

To Students

Living at home and commuting when you don't want to is a drag. What can you do? You can work on a plan for moving out, and at the same time, try to make your commuting life easier.

1. Don't Self-Destruct.

If you feel like you're stuck at home, then you might feel desperate enough to assert your autonomy any way you can—even if it means failing school or harming your body through starvation or alcohol abuse. Although these self-destructive processes are mostly unconscious, you can catch yourself in the act and stop them. The situation is not worth hurting yourself over. Besides, you'll just end up with less freedom because you'll be inviting your parents to hover over you even more. It's well worth your demonstrating how responsible and mature you can be, so that when the time comes for you to make your breakout independence move, they won't have any good reason to try and stop you.

2. Making a Departure Plan.

You have to decide how important it is to you to move out. Is it worth your spending the time looking into alternative funding options, including getting a job? Is it worth your potentially bearing the brunt of your parents' anger for a few weeks, maybe even months? If so, read on.

   a. Do your research. You may suspect that your parents are more capable of financial support than they let on. Even so, if you're going to make a move that goes against their wishes, it's best to first see whether or not you'll be able to cover your tracks with loans, scholarships, and employment.

   b. Sit your parents down.

- Let them know exactly how commuting is putting wear and tear on your academic and social lives, as well as your relationship with them. Let them know that in order to stop resentment from growing and to put good will and warm feelings back into the parent-child relationships, it's best that you move out.
- Empathize that you know this is hard for them to deal with, but that you weighed everything and decided that commuting was costing you more in terms of your life than leaving would cost them emotionally.
- If they embrace the move, then involve them in the problem-solving phase.
- Let them know how you plan to cover the extra expense, but that you would welcome any assistance they want to offer.

- Say that you thought that they might even be proud of you for realizing what you need to succeed at school and going after it.
- Tell them that you'd like to consult them on a timetable. If you can honestly give them two or three options to choose from, that's great, such as, "I could stay with my friends in the dorm starting in two weeks, or I could wait until the beginning of next semester."

c. Brace yourself for their anger and persuasive powers. Know that despite all the irrational guilt flooding you, you are not doing anything wrong, and that your parents will calm down eventually; they love you and want a relationship with you.

d. If you would like to move out but don't feel that it's financially feasible or that you are able to face your parents, consult a counselor on campus. Campus therapists are used to speaking with commuters who feel stuck in an uncomfortable situation. She or he will help you evaluate your situation and strategize on the best ways to improve the quality of your life.

3. **Making the Campus a Second Home.**

a. Find a convenient study spot on campus. If there's no library near your classes, then how about an empty classroom or a quiet café? If the café isn't so quiet, then bring along earplugs or a Walkman. Building regular hangouts into your routine can help you structure your time and be productive.

b. For the times when you don't need to be in class or study, put yourself where people socialize: the student union, a popular set of steps or stretch of lawn, or a sandwich shop. If you recognize somebody from class or an activity, then you can use the opening line, "I think you're in my bio class; what do you think of it so far?"

c. Join *at least* one club on campus. Check out a few at first and see which have people with whom you click. If you have an old hobby that you lost sight of, pick it up again. Take a dance or gym class.

d. Lugging all of your textbooks and notepads can be quite a hassle. If you don't have a car that you drive to campus everyday and can store things in, then try to get a locker on campus. Perhaps offer a friend some homework help in exchange for a little storage space; with roommates around though, this can get kind of tricky.

e. Find a crash pad at school, both for late-night socializing and study sessions.

Of course you don't want to overstay your welcome on somebody's floor; but if it's a good friend, he might even welcome the company.

4. Gaining Privacy and Autonomy at Home.

Brainstorm on how you can create more personal space. Here are a few general suggestions that you may or may not want to follow depending on your personality.

a. Get your own phone line. A cell phone would be great but talking for a lot of hours can get quite expensive.

b. Exercise your right to shut the door to your room.

c. Decide how you want to handle staying out late. You might prefer calling your parents if you won't be back by a certain hour as opposed to always letting them know exactly where you're going.

d. Whether or not you bring friends and dates home should be at your discretion. Yet, I wouldn't count on being able to have a romantic partner stay the night.

EPILOGUE

Bringing Home the Laundry Revisited

Remember the college student who dragged her dirty clothes through a big city for two hours to wash her laundry at home, with her mother's socks? By now, you've probably guessed that this laundry dance had something to do with change resistance. The mother, feeling stuck in an unhappy marriage, had hoped that the daughter—to whom she was close—would live at home for college. The daughter chose to live on campus, but worried guiltily that her mother would feel abandoned. Unconsciously, she chose laundry visits as a way to reassure her mother that she still loved her.

Cleaning clothes shouldn't be so complicated. Here are general laundering guidelines depending upon where your family falls on the assisting change scale:

Change Resisters

Parents—Coach your child on laundering, but don't get your hands wet.
Students—Wash your laundry yourself at school, and leave your parents a phone message, "I just did my own laundry and am proud to report that at least half my clothes still fit me."

Change Assisters

Parents—Your instincts are good—follow them.

Students—It's never too soon to learn to do your own wash; you might run out of underwear and socks during finals and have to do an emergency load.

Change Desisters

Parents—Invite your child over for laundry washing and tea and cookies. Feeding your child is always a good idea; food equals nurturance.

Students—If you live nearby, make regular, predictable trips home to do your laundry, but bring your own laundry detergent. If you want to see a look of pleasant shock on your parents' faces, then offer to wash their sheets and towels.

Commuters

Parents—Launch your child from the nest by giving him laundry lessons, so that you can feel reassured that he will survive out there on his own.

Students—Do your own laundry as one of the many signs to your parents that you're ready for independence. Hide your laundering mistakes. Don't do the family's wash—if you do, then they'll never let you leave.

Remember, laundry isn't the only tie that binds families together. Now that your child has moved out of the house, you're both free to connect on new, exciting ground. Research has shown that assisting change during the college years helps conflicted families get along better and helps happy families become happier. There is only one direction to go from here, and that's a good one.

Use this opportunity for all it's worth. Pat yourself on the back for launching your child to college and for working toward making your relationship as strong as it can be. Apply the actions recommended in the book to the real world, and then six months from now, re-take the Change Resistance Test to see how far you've come. These can honestly be some of the best years of your life.

APPENDIX

Helpful Books, Web Sites, and Hotlines

Financing a College Education

Kalman, Chany A. and Geoff Martz. *Paying for College Without Going Broke (2000 ed.)*, Vol. 1. New York: Princeton Review Publ. Corp., 1999.

Krefetz, Gerald. *The Parents' Guide to Paying for College: Practical Strategies and Financial Guidelines to Covering College Costs.* New York: College Entrance Examination Board/The College Board, 1999.

Peterson's Staff. *Peterson's Scholarship Almanac: Including the 500 Largest Scholarships to Help Pay for College.* New Jersey: Peterson's, 1998.

Surf the Internet for sites guiding you to special scholarships and loans:

- collegescholarships.com
- collegedegree.com
- embark.com

Sex Information

Bell, Ruth. *Changing Bodies, Changing Lives: A Book for Teens on Sex and Relationships*. New York: Times Books, 1998.

Boston Women's Health Group Collective. *New Our Bodies, Ourselves*. New York: Simon and Schuster, 1998.

- CDC National STD and AIDS Hotlines and Web Sites:
  (800) 342-AIDS (800-342-2437) and http://www.ashastd.org/nah/nah.html
- Planned Parenthood, Inc. (800) 829-7732 (Regular weekday hours)
  or (800) 230-7526 (24-hour automated service) and
  http://www.plannedparenthood.org or teenwire.com.
- The Gay and Lesbian National Hotline:
  (888) 843-4564 (Monday through Fridays 6 P.M. to 10 P.M., Saturday noon to
  5 P.M.) and E-mail: glnh.org.

Drug and Alcohol Information

Hicks, John. *Drug Addiction: No Way I'm An Addict*, Brookfield, CT: Millbrook Press, 1997.

Huard, Donald V. *Teenagers: What Will Cigarettes, Booze, "Safe" Sex and Drugs Do for You?* Huard Publishers, 1997.

Drug Help (For alcohol or drugs): 1-800-378-4435 (twenty-four hours: counseling, answer questions, and referrals for counselors near you.) www.drughelp.org

Alcohol and Drug Referral Line:

(800) 821-4357 (twenty-four hours: Referrals to a local counselor for any issues concerning alcohol or drug use.)

Alcoholics Anonymous (AA) and Narcotics Anonymous (NA):

Look in your local phone book or call directory assistance for the branch nearest you. (212) 647-1680 (twenty-four hours, but *not* toll-free: a recovering alcoholic is there to speak with you.)

Web site: http://www.alcoholics-anonymous.org

American Cancer Society Smoker Quitline:

(800) 227-2345 (twenty-four hours: Referrals to local quitting programs and information on smoking's dangers and how to quit.)

Web site: http://www.cancer.org

http://stopdrugs.org: Deals with both prevention and treatment of drug-related problems.

http://www.alcoholismhelp.com: Provides help with alcoholism.

Study Tips Online

thenode.canlearn.ca/studybuddy.shtml

studyweb.com

homeworkcentral.com.

Spicing Up Sex in a Longterm Marriage

Comfort, Alex, et al. *The New Joy of Sex (The Joy of Sex Series)*. New York: Pocket Books, 1992.

Danielou, Alain (Translator). *The Complete Kama Sutra: The First Unabridged Modern Translation of the Classic Indian Text*. Rochester, VT: Inner Traditions Intl. Ltd., 1995.

Gottman, John, and Nan Silver. *Why Marriages Succeed or Fail: And How You Can Make Yours Last*. New York: Fireside, 1995.

Love, Dr. Patricia, et al. *Hot Monogamy: Essential Steps to More Passionate, Intimate Lovemaking*. New York: Plume, 1999.

Schnarch, David. *Passionate Marriage: Love, Sex, and Intimacy in Emotionally Committed Relationships*. New York: W. W. Norton & Co., 1997.

Schwartz, Pepper, Ph.D., and Janet Lever, Ph.D. *The Great Sex Weekend: A 48-Hour Guide to Rekindling Sparks for Bold, Busy, or Bored Lovers: Includes 24-Hour Plans for the Really Busy*. New York: Putnam Pub. Group, 1998.

Webb, Michael. *The RoMANtic's Guide: Hundreds of Creative Tips for a Lifetime of Love*. New York: Hyperion, 2000.

Late-Start Career Inspiration

Rent the movie *Music of the Heart*, directed by Wes Craven, starring Meryl Streep. The story is based on the life of a real woman who, after being left by her husband, entered the workforce with little experience and created an incredibly fulfilling life for herself. There's also the documentary film covering the same story, entitled *Small Wonders*.

WORKS CITED

Attiz, Thomas. *How We Grieve: Relearning the World*. Oxford, New York: Oxford University Press, 1996.

Barkin, Carol. *When Your Kid Goes to College: A Parent's Survival Guide*. New York: Avon Books, 1999.

Bowlby, John. *Separation: Anxiety and Anger*. New York: Basic Books Inc., 1973.

Brady, Lois Smith. "VOWS: AN UPDATE; The Seven-Year Itch: Where Are They Now?" *New York Times*, 2 May 1999.

Chiu, Christina. *Eating Disorder: Survivors Tell Their Stories (The Teen Health Library of Eating Disorder Prevention)*. New York: The Rosen Publishing Group, Inc., 1998.

Contemporary Issues Companion. *Eating Disorders*. Ed. by Myra H. Immell. California: Greenhaven Press, Inc., 1999.

Cowan, Carolyn Pape, and Philip A. Cowan. *When Partners Become Parents: The Big Life Change for Couples*. Mahwah, NJ: Lawrence Erlbaum Associates, Inc., 2000.

Duyff, Roberta Larson. *The American Dietetic Association's Complete Food and Nutrition Guide*. New York: John Wiley & Sons, 1998.

http://www.detnews.com/1999/food/0603/tomato/tomato.htm

FinAid. *FinAid! The SmartStudent Guide to Financial Aid.* Finaid Page LLC, http://www.finaid.org

Hinds, Jeanne. *E-mail to* http://patriot.net/~crouch/adr/50percent.html

Hobson, Sally. *Chicken Little.* New York: Simon and Schuster, 1994.

Hochschild, Arlie, and Anne Machung. *The Second Shift.* New York: William Morrow & Co., 1990.

Indiana Jones: The Last Crusade. Dir. Steven Speilberg. Perf. Harrison Ford and Sean Connery. Paramount, 1989.

Kubler-Ross, Elisabeth. *Death: The Final Stage of Growth.* New York: Simon & Schuster, 1975.

Louis, David. *2201 Fascinating Facts.* New York: Wings Books, 1983.

Minuchin, Salvador. *Families of the Slums.* New York: Basic Books, 1967.

———. *Fresh Air*, National Public Radio, 28 March 1990.

National Center for Health Statistics. "Advance Report of Final Divorce Statistics, 1989 and 1990 Monthly Vital Statistics Report, Vol. 43, No. 9, Supplement For Release April 18, 1995." *Centers for Disease Control and Prevention–NCHS.*
http://www.cdc.gov/nchs/releases/95facts/95sheets/fs_439s.htm

Pasick, Patricia, M. Ed., Ph.D. *Almost Grown: Launching Your Child from High School to College.* New York: W. W. Norton & Company, 1998.

Viorst, Judith. *Necessary Losses.* New York: Simon & Schuster, 1986.

Vladeck, Andrew. "The Wheel Came Full Circle (And It Ran Me Over)." Full-Tilt Records, 1999.

Wilgoren, Jodi. "Life 101: Useful Skills for College and Beyond." *New York Times*, 15 October 1999, A1.

INDEX